Mr Mitchell

THE GOBSMACKING GALAXY

Other books in The Knowledge series:

Flaming Olympics
by Michael Coleman

Potty Politics
by Terry Deary

Foul Football
by Michael Coleman

Murderous Maths
by Kjartan Poskitt

Look out for:

Groovy Movies
by Martin Oliver

Awful Art
by Michael Cox

THE GOBSMACKING GALAXY

KJARTAN POSKITT

Illustrated by

Daniel Postgate

Hippo

To Patrick Moore CBE – the only person whose autograph
I have ever asked for. Without his inspired programmes and
books, millions of people would never have got interested
in the galaxy.

Scholastic Children's Books,
Commonwealth House, 1–19 New Oxford Street,
London WC1A 1NU, UK
A division of Scholastic Limited
London ~ New York ~ Toronto ~ Sydney ~ Auckland
Mexico City ~ New Delhi ~ Hong Kong

Published in the UK by Scholastic Ltd, 1997
Text copyright © Kjartan Poskitt, 1997
Illustrations copyright © Daniel Postgate, 1997

ISBN 0 590 19013 X

Typeset by TW Typesetting, Midsomer Norton, Avon
Printed by Cox & Wyman Ltd, Reading, Berks

11 13 15 17 19 20 18 16 14 12

The right of Kjartan Poskitt and Daniel Postgate to be identified as the author and
illustrator of this work respectively has been asserted by them in accordance
with the Copyright, Designs and Patents Act, 1988.

Contents

WARNING!

BEFORE READING THIS BOOK
YOU MUST
PREPARE YOUR BRAIN

Why?

Because what you are about to find out is so mind-bogglingly amazing that your jaw might drop off and hit the floor. Of course, it wouldn't be so bad if this was just a made up story book, but what's really freaky is that EVERYTHING IN THIS BOOK IS TRUE! It's completely gobsmacking.

Just to give you an idea of what your head is going to have to deal with, imagine looking up on a clear dark night. The stars are pretty awesome on their own, but what about the black area behind them? What is it? Who put it there? How far away is it? And the freakiest question of all ... is there anything on the other side?

Even the cleverest people can only guess the answer, but this book is going to take you out there so you can decide for yourself!

Be ready to grit your teeth, though, because along the way it isn't just pretty little stars twinkling away! In fact, this is your guide to:

THE GOBSMACKING GALAXY!

WHAT IS A GALAXY ANYWAY?

Galaxy is the name given to lots of different bits flying about together in space. Galaxies can be different shapes, some are just blobbish, and others (like ours) are nice spirals.

How to make a model of our galaxy at dinner time

- You need a bowl of oxtail soup, and some cream.
- Stir the oxtail soup so that it's going round the bowl.
- While it's still moving, pour a long dribble of cream across the soup.
- You should get a spiral shape very similar to our galaxy.

There are only two important differences. One is that our galaxy is MUCH bigger. The other is that it doesn't taste of oxtail soup.

Later on in this book there will be more about the galaxy as a whole and how it fits in with other galaxies and why the universe is expanding at the speed of light but then might collapse to the size of an atom in a massive physical singularity which distorts time itself...

...but I don't think we're quite ready for that yet, are we?

No, first things first: let's find out what the

different bits are that the galaxy is made up of.

- By the way, we will be meeting some very big numbers, in particular there are a lot of BILLIONS. In this book a BILLION is the same as one thousand million, or 1,000,000,000.
- We will also be talking about different temperatures. All temperatures are in degrees Centigrade, or °C. Just to give you a guide:

0° is when water freezes

100°C is when water boils

25°C is a nice warm day

250°C is when paper catches fire

MINUS 273°C is absolute zero ... the coldest temperature possible!

The contents of a galaxy

Obviously, we can't mention EVERYTHING here such as ants, socks, kebab shops and so on, but this is a rough list of what's flying about in space starting with the biggest bits:

Stars

Our galaxy contains about a million million stars and these are the biggest single items in space. They can vary in size, temperature and age but they are all burning away furiously producing heat and light, which is how we can see them.

Solar system

Our solar system includes our own personal star which we call the Sun, and the planets and other bits that are flying round it. (The word solar means "to do with the Sun".) The Sun is only a smallish star but don't be disappointed. If it

had been any bigger we would all have been frazzled up eons ago.

Planets

Orbiting round our Sun is a set of planets. (We've just discovered planets going round some other stars, too.) The Sun is far bigger than all its planets together, and also planets do not generate light, we can only see them because the Sun lights them up.

Satellites (or moons)

"Satellite" can mean all sorts of things but basically it's a smaller thing that latches on to a bigger thing otherwise it doesn't know where to go.

(If ever you get to be a big pop star you'll find you have loads of satellites, although they call themselves public relations executives, agents and image consultants.) Earth has one natural satellite, the Moon, which spins round the Earth and so

wherever the Earth goes the Moon comes too. Earth also has thousands of unnatural satellites; these are man-made things like space stations and satellite dishes and general space junk. Some planets don't have any moons, and some have a lot more than their fair share, as you will see later.

Comets

Comets are fab. While everything else in the solar system generally toddles round keeping out of everybody else's way, comets hurl themselves from one side of the solar system to the other and back again. This is even cleverer when you

know that your average comet is just a five-mile-wide ice cube.

Asteroids

These are lumps of rock and metal flying about in space. In the solar system most of them are in "The Asteroid Belt" which runs between Mars and Jupiter. The biggest asteroid in the belt is 1,000 km across, and nobody knows how  small the smallest is because it's too small. (The great thing about space is that there's a lot of stuff that nobody knows, so you can make something up and nobody can definitely say you're wrong. You could even say the smallest asteroid is made of jam and speaks French and nobody could prove you were lying.)

Meteorites

Nasty! These are generally runaway asteroids or comets which come crashing down to Earth. They get so hot that they burn up as they plummet through the atmosphere and consequently they are a lot smaller by the time  they hit the ground. That's a relief because, to give an idea of how powerful they are, millions of years ago a meteorite hit Canada and made a crater 4km across! The biggest meteorite found on Earth is 55 tonnes and it landed in the African country of Namibia, so it's amazing that Namibia is still there. Some people think that a massive meteorite hit the Earth 65 million years ago and the general mess, noise and chaos caused the dinosaurs to die out. Either that or all the dinosaurs climbed up into a big pile and the meteorite came down and squashed the LOT.

Meteors

These are tiny little specks of dust usually left behind by comets and they burn up completely when they enter the Earth's atmosphere. They are nicknamed shooting stars and if you look up at a clear sky in the first two weeks of  August, be patient and you might see a few. Even though they are tiny, if one hits a space rocket it can do a lot of damage because in space everything travels irresponsibly fast. (Even YOU do – as you read this, you're flying round the Sun at more than 100,000 km/h. Hold on tight!)

Well, that's the general list of lumps and bumps that we're sharing the galaxy with.

Later on we are going to take a trip right across the galaxy which means we will have to go...

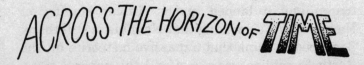

Oo-er ... that sounds a bit dramatic, doesn't it?

Actually it isn't because the first thing to realize about space is that everything is a very long way away. To get to the edge of the galaxy is going to take squillions of years so when we plan to go there, we'll have to slow time down. Impossible, eh? Well maybe not, but we'll come to that later when your brain is more ready for it.

Let's keep things really simple to start with, and what could be simpler than this:

1 Wait for a nice clear dark night.
2 Turn off all your lights and open the curtains. (Or better still, go outside.)
3 Look up.
4 Look at the next page in this book. (You can turn the light on and look down again while you are doing this.)

WHAT CAN YOU SEE?

If you didn't know any better, you would say there
are only three different things you can see in the sky
(not counting Earth things, like clouds, aeroplanes,
lost balloons, escaped budgies and so on).

1 The Sun
2 The Moon
3 Stars

The Sun

Obviously, the Sun is the brightest object we ever
see in our sky because the Sun is our nearest STAR.
It behaves like a massive burning ball of fuel which
is why it sends out so much heat and light. You'll
find out more about this later on in the book unless
you are a very slow reader. (The Sun is due to burn
out in $4\frac{1}{2}$ billion years so hurry up.) The Sun is the
centre point of our solar system and Earth orbits
round it in a big circle once a year.

Why do you think we don't see the Moon or any
stars in daytime?

1 They all switch themselves off to conserve fuel.
2 The blue sky gets in the way.
3 The Sun is SO bright it dazzles us from seeing
  them even though they are there all the time.
4 They all go and hide round the back of the Earth
  where you can't see them.

  ● The answer is a combination of 2 and 3. The strong
  sunlight coming through the atmosphere makes it
  look blue and blocks our view. As the Sun sets and
  the sky darkens the brighter objects start to appear,
  until when the Sun's gone you can see everything.

15

The Moon

ALL ABOUT THE MOON
by K. Poskitt
The Moon is just a big potato floating in the sky,
And little men from outer space are often passing by.
When they're feeling hungry they might eat a bit
for dinner,
That's why the Moon is sometimes fat, and other
times it's thinner.

The Moon is the second brightest thing in the sky but it isn't nearly as bright as the Sun. This is because the Moon is just a big round rock and the Sun has to shine on it before we can see it.

The Moon orbits around Earth once every 28 days but not quite in a perfect circle. Although its average distance from us is about 384,000 km, it can come as close as 356,000 km or go as far away as 407,000 km.

Three magic tricks!
Between them, the Sun and the Moon create some good optical illusions.

Trick number one

They both look about the same size, but in reality:

the Sun is 1,400,000 km across

the Moon is 3,500 km across!

… so the Sun is 400 times bigger than the Moon!
However:

the Sun is 150,000,000 km away

the Moon is 384,000 km away

… so the Sun is about 400 times further away! This strange coincidence means that they appear to be the same size.

● In the same way that the Moon and Sun look the same size, you can make a coin look the same size as a house. Stand a few hundred metres away from the house and hold up your coin at arm's length. Of course the coin and the house will look about the same size!

Trick number two

The Moon seems to change shape! You have probably noticed that sometimes the Moon is a full round circle and at other times it is only half a circle or even just a crescent shape.

FULL MOON

CRESCENT MOON

So where has the rest of the Moon gone?

Of course, it hasn't gone anywhere but, like any good illusionist, it uses a trick of the light to disappear.

You can try this trick for yourself. You need a torch, something round like a ball and you need to be in a dark room.

First hold the torch out in front of you and shine it on the ball. Of course you will see the full round shape of the ball. This is like when we see a full Moon, it's because the Sun is shining directly on to it.

Now lie the torch down at the side of the ball but then come back and stand where you were. The torch is only lighting up one side of the ball and so it looks like you only have half a ball! When we see half a Moon it is because the sunlight is coming from the side.

If you move the torch a little bit further round to the back of the ball you will get the effect of a crescent Moon.

Trick number three

Finally, the Sun and Moon occasionally play a very special trick called an ECLIPSE. This is when the Moon and Earth cast shadows on each other in the sunlight.

There are two sorts of eclipse. A lunar eclipse is when the Moon disappears and a solar eclipse is when the Sun disappears.

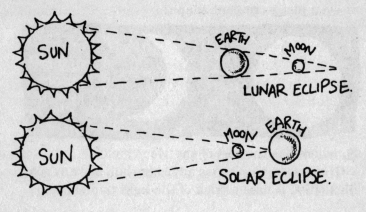

LUNAR ECLIPSE.

SOLAR ECLIPSE.

LUNAR ECLIPSE: Sometimes when the Moon goes round the Earth it passes through Earth's shadow, which blocks the sunlight off. This means that one minute you are looking at a full Moon but then slowly you see a round black shape creeping across it (this shape is the Earth's shadow).

Ancient Chinese people had another explanation for a lunar eclipse: the Moon was being swallowed by a giant three-legged toad.

Sometimes the shadow only slightly covers the Moon and this is called a PARTIAL ECLIPSE. At other times the shadow completely engulfs the Moon and this is a TOTAL ECLIPSE.

- A lunar eclipse can last up to a couple of hours.
- There are usually one or two lunar eclipses every year.
- During a full eclipse the Moon rather mysteriously takes on a dark reddish-gold colour. This is because although the Earth is stopping direct sunlight reaching the Moon, the redder colours in sunlight are deflected by the atmosphere around the Earth. Some of this red light can hit the Moon – and it looks brilliant!

SOLAR ECLIPSE: Sometimes the Moon moves directly between the Sun and the Earth, casting a shadow on the Earth. If you are standing on Earth where the shadow falls you will see the Moon moving in front of the Sun and blocking out the light. This is a solar eclipse.

There are three types of solar eclipse. A TOTAL ECLIPSE is when the Moon completely blocks the

Sun out. A PARTIAL ECLIPSE is when the Moon gets slightly in the way. An ANNULAR ECLIPSE happens when the Moon is at its furthest distance away from us and so appears just a bit too small to completely cover the Sun.

TOTAL ECLIPSE   PARTIAL ECLIPSE   ANNULAR ECLIPSE

- Total solar eclipses can only be seen from a small part of the Earth. People a hundred miles away may only see a partial eclipse, and thousands of miles away it might not be possible to see any eclipse at all.
- There are anything between two and five solar eclipses a year.
- You should be able to see a total solar eclipse from your own house about once every four hundred years – but watch carefully because they only last a few minutes!
- In ancient times people used to be terrified by solar eclipses. During an eclipse not only does the Sun seem to disappear in the middle of the day, but the temperature gets chilly, the wind drops and everything gets a bit spooky!
- Total solar eclipses are very special occasions for scientists. For just a few short minutes they get a

chance to examine how the Sun works and all sorts of other weird physical curiosities such as how light bends and time distorts!

● Just as the Moon is covering up the last bit of sunlight, brilliant points of pink light appear round its edge. This is the sunlight beaming through the valleys on the Moon. During a total eclipse, massive blasts of light come out from behind the black disc of the Moon – these blasts are called the Sun's CORONA.

● Solar eclipses are so spectacular that there are a whole lot of people who spend all their money and holidays travelling round the world trying to see every single one. If ever you get a chance to see a solar eclipse, don't miss it!

The stars ... and other things!

Ancient people were fascinated by the night sky and spent a lot of time trying to map it out. They imagined the stars formed patterns in the sky, and they gave these patterns names. The posh word for these star patterns is "constellations" and there are 88 of them.

Can you match these eight names with their constellations? (Constellations are usually drawn with lines connecting their main stars, but of course

21

you can't see the lines in the sky. If you *can* see the lines then you are WEIRD.)

Orion "the Hunter"
Leo "the Lion"
Ursa Major "the Great Bear"
Cygnus "the Swan"
Pegasus "the Flying Horse"
Taurus "the Bull"
Aquila "the Eagle"
Auriga "the Charioteer"

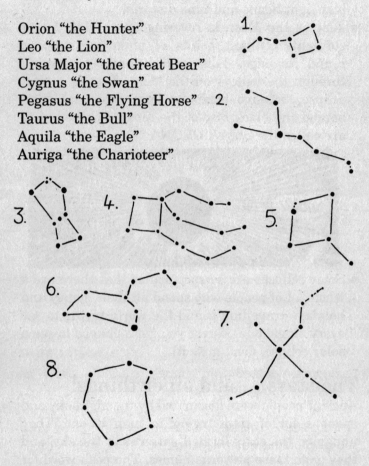

Did you find that difficult? Don't worry, it's a complete mystery how anybody could have thought these patterns look even remotely like their names. How about this one...

Unbelievable, isn't it? There is only one way to explain how the ancients could see animals and people in the sky: all that staying up late at night must have softened their brains.

● The constellations we use are based on the system laid out by the Greek astronomer Ptolemy in the second century AD. He took most of the constellation names from myths and legends. More modern constellation names are not nearly as exciting. How about Antlia "the Air Pump"!

Joking aside, the ancients actually did a very good job of plotting out the stars, but they soon noticed that a few of the twinkling objects did not stay in the same places. These wandering stars caused a lot of concern and became known as the planets, which means "wanderers". They used to worship them as gods riding about in the heavens, but these days we think we know better.

The planets

Apart from wandering about, what's the difference between planets and stars?

- Planets are a LOT closer to us and orbit round the Sun, just like Earth does.
- Planets are extremely tiny compared to stars.
- Planets don't shine with their own light, they just reflect light from the Sun.

Ancient people identified five planets (other than Earth): Mercury, Venus, Mars, Jupiter and Saturn. Together this made seven independent objects in the sky (counting the Sun and Moon too), which made sense to them as they thought seven was a magical number.

For thousands of years these were the only planets anyone knew about. That was until 1781 when Sir William Herschel happened to find Uranus. Suddenly seven was not such a mystical number!

In 1846 Neptune was discovered, and in 1930 Pluto was seen for the first time.

What is astrology?

Of the 88 constellations, 12 are called the signs of the zodiac or "star signs". Do you know which one is yours? It depends when your birthday is:

Aries, "the Ram"	21 March–20 April
Taurus, "the Bull"	21 April–21 May
Gemini, "the Twins"	22 May–21 June
Cancer, "the Crab"	22 June–23 July
Leo, "the Lion"	24 July–23 August
Virgo, "the Virgin"	24 August–23 September
Libra, "the Scales"	24 September–23 October
Scorpio, "the Scorpion"	24 October–22 November
Sagittarius, "the Archer"	23 November–21 December
Capricorn, "the Goat"	22 December–20 January
Aquarius, "the Water-carrier"	21 January–19 February
Pisces, "the Fish"	20 February–20 March

How do we know who gets which sign?

If the Sun was not so bright we would be able to see stars in the daytime as well as at night. The signs of the zodiac are based on the constellations that would be behind the Sun. During the year the Sun moves round the 12 zodiac constellations in turn, and as you can see from the list, it takes about a month to pass through each one. For instance, on 15 May the Sun is in front of Taurus, but by 3 June it has moved into Gemini.

Unfortunately there is a slight complication with the 12 signs. Since the olden days when the zodiac was first arranged, the way the stars have been divided up into constellations has been altered. Astrologers still use the old system, but with the modern system, instead of passing straight from Scorpio into Sagittarius, the Sun actually goes through a 13th constellation called Ophiuchus, "the Serpent-bearer". If your birthday is around 20 November you are really an Ophiuchian!

ASTROLOGERS are very different from ASTRONOMERS. Astronomers study the sky and find out real things that we did not know.

Astrologers also study the sky very carefully (and a lot of them are very good at it), but they expect you to believe that your character and your luck depend on which "star sign" you were born under. They get very excited if any planets are passing through your constellation, and they make silly predictions in the newspaper such as "Capricorn: A day of truths but don't give way in matters of the heart" or "Leo: Matters may come to a head today, a time for change beckons".

26

Can your star sign really make any difference to you?

No, of course it can't. A few burning gas balls billions of miles away don't matter a diddle to anyone – you are far more likely to be affected by a pigeon flying overhead.

It can be quite fun getting two or three different newspapers on one day and seeing the horoscopes that have been made up for you. Sometimes they are all different which shows that it's complete drivel.

So is astrology a waste of time?

NO! It's clean harmless fun and gives us all something silly to talk about. Hooray.

- If you want to see your own sign of the zodiac in the sky, it's no good looking on your birthday because the Sun will dazzle it out of view! The best time to look is 6 months after your birthday when your star sign will be on the other side of the sky from the Sun, so it appears at night. Gemini, Taurus, Virgo and Leo are the easiest of the zodiac constellations to spot, but it isn't too hard to find the others if you try.

SKY SPOTTING: HOW TO GET STARTED

This book is all you need to start finding out about the sky, but if you have a couple of pounds to spare you will also find it very helpful to have a proper map of the stars. A good bookshop should be able to sell you a star chart or a guide book which will show you where all the constellations are, what some of the main stars are called, and might even indicate where you will see the planets. Just to get you started, on the last two pages of this book are two simple star charts to show you the main constellations.

A REALLY good bookshop might be able to sell you a planisphere, which is a round map with a dial on it. When you turn the dial it shows you exactly which stars you can see for any time of any night of the year. (Although it is called a PLANIsphere, unfortunately it cannot show you the planets!)

What you can see depends where on Earth you are and what time of year it is.

29

The brightness of stars

The brightness of a star as it appears to us is called its MAGNITUDE. Funnily enough, it works the wrong way round because the brighter a star is, the lower the number.

Here are some typical magnitudes:

- 10 Extremely faint star, you'll need a big telescope.
- 6 The faintest stars you can see with the naked eye.

0   A very bright star.

-1.6   This is the magnitude of Sirius, the brightest star in the sky.

-4.4   This is the maximum brightness of the planet Venus.

-12.5   This is the full Moon.

-26.7   This is the brightness of the Sun.

● From Earth, Sirius appears to be the brightest star in the sky, but Sirius is quite near – only 8½ light years away. Other stars are far more powerful than Sirius (such as Rigel in Orion) but they are much further away so they don't seem so bright to us.

How to find the planets

Because the planets move about the sky, it is almost impossible to mark them on a map.

There are exceptions. Various "almanacs" and charts are printed on a yearly basis, and one of the best is a little book called *The Times Night Sky*. This has a map specially drawn up for each month of that year and it shows where the planets are. It also tells you where the Moon is going to be and if there are going to be any good eclipses.

You can have fun spotting the planets yourself! Once you've got used to the different star constellations, look out and see if any of them have suddenly got an extra star. (Make sure it isn't an aeroplane or a flying saucer or anything.) This will not be a star, it will be one of the planets.

Because of the way the planets move, some weeks there won't be any planets to see at all, but at other times you may see a few of them at once.

31

The inferior planets

Mercury and Venus are called the inferior planets. Does this mean that they are sad, humble little things that could be bossed around by a goldfish? No, it just means that they are closer to the Sun than Earth. Because they are near the Sun, they are always in the sky during the day, but of course during the day the Sun dazzles them from view, making them pretty well impossible to see. However, if they are in the right place, we sometimes do get a chance to see them shortly before sunrise or just after sunset.

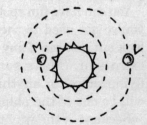

FROM EARTH, MERCURY AND VENUS ALWAYS APPEAR NEAR THE SUN. THIS MEANS WE NEVER SEE THEM AT NIGHT.

If Mercury and Venus have moved round so that they are in line with the Sun then we don't have a chance of seeing them at all. (Being in line with the Sun is called "conjunction".)

In this diagram Mercury is between us and the Sun, so you might think you should be able to see it. In fact it would be like trying to spot a grain of sand on a distant car's headlight.

When Mercury and
Venus are to one side
of the Sun or the
other, they can then
be seen either just
before the Sun comes
up in the morning or
just after the Sun
sets in the evening.

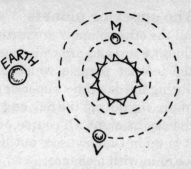

Even when it is in the best position for viewing,
Mercury can only be seen in the two hours before
sunrise or two hours after sunset. Unfortunately it
is quite difficult to find because it is small and
always down near the horizon. (It is harder to see
things low down in the sky because the air near the
ground shimmers and tends to make details hazy.)

Venus is further away from the Sun than Mercury
so it can be seen up to three hours before sunrise or
up to three hours after sunset. In most months it is
easy to find – either leading the Sun over the
eastern horizon in the early morning or following
the Sun down in the west in the evening. It is nearly
always the brightest thing in the sky – not counting
the Sun and Moon, of course.

In ancient times people thought Venus was two
different stars. When it appeared at sunrise, it was
called "The Morning Star" or even "Lucifer", and
when it appeared at sunset it was called "The
Evening Star" or "Hesperus".

If you look at Venus with good binoculars or a
telescope, you will see it can have different phases,
just like the Moon – sometimes you might only see a
crescent shape and at others you see the whole planet.

The superior planets

All the other planets are further away from the Sun than we are and are called superior planets. Unlike the inferior planets which are always in the sky during the day time, superior planets are sometimes in the sky during the day and sometimes they are in the sky at night. Of course, we can't see a planet if it is up in the daytime, but if it is up at night-time we're in with a chance.

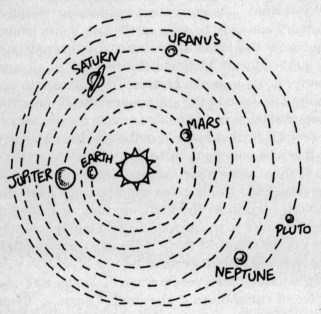

This diagram is just a very rough picture of how Earth and the superior planets go round the Sun – there wasn't room to fit Mercury and Venus in. Most of the circles should be a lot bigger but unless this book was the size of a bus, we wouldn't fit them on the page!

Remember the Earth is spinning round all the time so sometimes we will be on the side facing the Sun (daytime), and 12 hours later we will be on the side facing away from the Sun (night-time).

The diagram shows Mars in conjunction (in line with the Sun). If we were on the right side of Earth to be looking at Mars, we would also be able to see the Sun – in other words it would be daytime so even though Mars is up there, we can't see it.

In this diagram Jupiter is being far more exciting because it is on the opposite side of the Earth from the Sun. (This position is called "opposition".) If we were on the right side of Earth to be looking at Jupiter, we would not be able to see the Sun at all – i.e. Jupiter is up in the darkest part of the night sky and is perfect for looking at.

If you want to show off how brainy this book has made you, say this to somebody:

MERCURY AND VENUS CAN NEVER BE IN OPPOSITION AND OF COURSE THIS IS WHY THEY ARE INFERIOR.

YOU WHAT?

The superior planets all travel round their orbits going from opposition to conjunction at different speeds, so the best time to see them is different for each one.

MARS spends about 14 months moving through conjunction and being hard or impossible to see. It then spends 12 months moving through opposition and becomes quite easy to see. Some oppositions are closer to us than others and during the best it can have a magnitude of −2.8, which makes it the second brightest thing in the sky after Venus. If you have a good stare at Mars you will realize it is quite orange in colour, which makes it easier to recognize when you see it again. If you make a point of trying to find Mars each night, you will see that it moves about quite a lot.

JUPITER comes into opposition about once every thirteen months and is always very bright, reaching a maximum magnitude of −2.6.

Through good binoculars or a proper telescope Jupiter looks much bigger than a pinpoint of light, and if you look very carefully you might be able to see Jupiter's four major moons if they are in the right place. (The moons orbit Jupiter quite quickly, so if you don't see them all on one night, try again a few nights later and you might be in luck.)

With a really good telescope you can see some of the markings on the planet, including the famous red spot.

SATURN comes into opposition once every 54 weeks and can reach a magnitude of 0.3, which makes it brighter than most stars. If you get a chance to look at it with a good telescope, Saturn is the most amazing thing to see because the rings make it so different from everything else.

URANUS, NEPTUNE and PLUTO, the outer three planets, come round about once a year, but you'll be lucky to see them. In theory you should be able to see Uranus using just your eyes, but at magnitude 5.8, it will be about the dimmest thing you will be able to make out. Neptune is just too far away unless you have a really good telescope, and as for Pluto ... you may as well look for a fly's footprint in a coal cellar. (Mind you, later in this book we'll take you to Pluto and you'll realize you aren't missing much.)

Do I need lots of posh gear?

Not really – apart from this book and your own eyes all you need are THICK SOCKS and a WARM COAT. (To get the best views you need to be outside on a clear night, and it can get pretty chilly!)

Of course you have to have trousers, pants, shirt, shoes and so on, too.

If you can get a proper star chart or a planisphere, so much the better.

● For the BEST view of the sky, you should be away from any lights, especially street lights. If you are lucky enough not to be in a town, the sky is always darker and clearer. Look up at the sky, wait for 2–3 minutes and as your eyes adjust it's amazing how more and more things appear. Try not to use a torch unless it is very dim.

If you find that you would like to explore the sky in more detail, then the best thing to do is borrow a pair of binoculars. Even a small pair will show you a lot more than you could ever see with just your naked eyes, and in particular you will see that some stars are different colours.

Once you've seen the sky through binoculars you will know if the subject has got you hooked. If it has then you might want to get some items of your own.

Telescopes

Do not buy a cheap telescope! One of those silly little things about 30cm long on a feeble stand is a complete waste of money – you would be far better off buying a pair of binoculars. A proper astronomical telescope will be a bit too expensive for most people, but there are other ways of getting a chance to look through one. There is probably an astronomical society in your area (your school might even have one), and people there should be able to arrange a visit to a proper observatory for you. They might even have an old telescope you can borrow or buy. It's worth asking!

WARNING!

You can look at anything you like in the night sky with binoculars or a telescope, but PLEASE do not ever look towards the Sun, even on a hazy day or during an eclipse. You will burn your eyes out!

This is the most important
thing you'll read in this book.

Books

There are lots of good books on astronomy, most of which are written by Patrick Moore. Some of them are specialized and deal with things like taking photographs or strange aspects of science, so have a flick through and find one or two that cover the topics you want to know about.

Camera

If you have a camera that lets you leave the shutter open, you can have fun experimenting with photographing the stars. Fix the camera to a tripod or stand it securely on something firm, then open the shutter and leave it still for an hour or so. When you get your pictures developed, the stars should appear as long streaks where they have moved across the sky. (If you don't get anything you might need a more sensitive film. Ask for advice at the photo shop.)

If you want to take REALLY classy pictures of objects in the sky (and a lot of the best things can only be seen by taking photographs), then life gets serious, complicated – and expensive! You will need a serious camera and a complicated motor drive fitted to an expensive telescope, and you will have to read up some serious, complicated and expensive books on the subject. Surprise, surprise – this isn't one of them!

SOME GOOD THINGS TO LOOK OUT FOR IN THE SKY

Once you've become familiar with the main constellations, you should find that you are able to spot Venus, Mars, Jupiter and Saturn whenever they are around.

Don't stop now! There are lots of other things to see if you can find them...

The Milky Way

If you look up on a clear night you might see what looks like a long thin mist going across the sky. You will realize that it is not a cloud because some stars will be shining in front of it. This "mist" is actually the rest of our own galaxy and is nicknamed "The Milky Way". Of course it isn't really a mist, what you are looking at is thousands of millions of stars stretching way out into space.

The Andromeda Galaxy

Our galaxy is just one of the millions and millions of galaxies that make up space. Our closest neighbour is the Andromeda Galaxy, and it is the furthest thing that can be seen with the naked eye. It is 20 million million million kilometres away, give or take a centimetre or two.

IF ... the night is absolutely clear and

IF ... you have perfect eyesight and

IF ... you are miles out in the country away from any lights and

IF ... there is no Moon and

IF ... you are looking in the right place

... you might just see a faint smudge in the sky.
That's it!

● Look for the Andromeda constellation (just below
Cassiopeia which is the big "W" shaped one), and
the galaxy is here:

Red and blue supergiants!

"Red Giant" is the name for a gigantic old star, and
you'll find out why later on in the book. One of the
biggest is Betelgeuse in Orion, even with your own
eyes you should be able to see that it is orange-red
rather than white. While you are studying Orion
notice Rigel too, this is one of the biggest and most
powerful stars in the sky and is a "Blue Supergiant".
(It is 57,000 times brighter than our Sun!) Other red

giants are Aldebaran in Taurus and Arcturus in Boötes.

Nebulas

A lot of astronomy books have brilliant pictures on the cover which look like massive blasts of fire in the sky – those are nebulas.

A nebula is a massive cloud of dust which is gradually coming together to form stars, and one of the best is the Great Nebula in Orion. Have a look – what do you see?

Yes, that's it. Unfortunately nebulas are a bit like fashion models. To look good they need decent lighting (most nebulas are lit by nearby stars) and they have to be photographed in the right way. Get it wrong and they often look fat and spotty. (The models, not the nebulas.) One particularly good nebula is called the Horsehead Nebula because in photographs it looks rather like a horse's head.

The Pleiades
This is a little bunch of stars nicknamed "The Seven Sisters" even though there are a lot more than seven of them. (A good test of your eyesight is how many stars you can see. Most people can pick out four or five, but the record is supposed to be 13!) They are very young and hot and the cluster is especially bright because of the nebula gas around them. With binoculars you might notice they are a blue-white colour, and many people think they are the prettiest sight in deep space. The Pleiades are close to the main stars in Taurus and look best around December.

Polaris
Polaris or the "Pole Star" or even the "North Star" is not one of the bigger stars, but for many people it is

the most important because it is always directly above the North Pole.

In the olden days Northern sailors used Polaris to help steer their ships at night, and many people still use it as a way of checking which way they are going. Polaris is the last star in the tail of Ursa Minor (The Little Bear). Two of the stars of Ursa Major always oint to it.

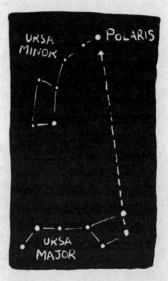

Although every other star in the sky moves around, Northerners will always find Polaris in the same place any time of night and at any time of the year.

The Coal Sack

This spooky dark patch is close to the South Pole, so it can only be seen in the Southern hemisphere. It's just an ordinary nebula but it does not have a nearby star to light it up, so it appears like a black cloud.

Comets

Comets fly in massive loops right across the solar system, and it's only when they come in close to the Sun that we can see them. This doesn't happen very often so when it does it's a bit special. As a comet approaches the Sun, it starts to glow and have a burning "tail" which can be millions of kilometres long. The funny thing is that the tail always points away from the Sun, so when the comet has passed the Sun and is flying back off into space, the tail sticks out in front. The reason they get called comets is because in olden days the Romans called them *stella cometa,* which means "hairy star". On some occasions they have been quite spectacular and in the olden days people could get quite frightened by these strange fuzzy stars that move across the sky.

There is a certain amount of risk involved in being a comet. They can crash into things and blow up, or sometimes they lose their orbit and go flying off for ever into deep space.

The most famous comet is Halley's comet, named after Edmund Halley who studied it in 1682. He made a careful note of its track and realized it was extremely similar to a comet seen in 1607 and another one before that in 1531. Halley realized that it was the same comet that was coming back to our end of the solar system about every 76 years and he predicted that it would return in 1758. He was right and it was spotted on the Christmas night of 1758, but sadly he didn't see it. Guess why...

- He was too busy playing with his Christmas presents.
- He had fallen to sleep after too much turkey.
- He forgot to look.
- He had died in 1742.

Once people had realized that Halley was right about his comet, old books and pictures were checked and people found records of it going back over two thousand years.

The last time Halley's comet came past this way was in 1986, but sadly it didn't get very close to us, although a few rockets were sent up to have a look and fly through its tail. The next visit in 2061 isn't supposed to be much better, but calculations show that in 2137 it should be well worth seeing, so write it in your diary now to remind you to have a look.

People get worried that Earth could be hit by a comet, but it is extremely unlikely. However, in 1994 Jupiter was hit by a comet going at 200,000 km/h and the crash blew up into explosions bigger than the Earth!

Meteors or "shooting stars"

These are tiny specks of dust that come into our atmosphere and burn up and look like – wait for it – shooting stars. They only last a few seconds but are dead cute to see. On any clear, dark night you could just lie out on a blanket and stare upwards, and you might be lucky enough to see one or two shooting stars.

There are also some especially good nights of the year when meteor showers regularly come down from the direction of particular constellations. Here are some of the best:

The Perseids

This shower lasts for the first two weeks of August and 12 August should be the best night of all. On a clear night find the constellation of Perseus and keep a lookout, you should be able to see about one every minute.

The Quadrantids

The first few nights of the year have a good shower, especially on 3 January. If you look between Ursa Major and Boötes you might see up to two meteors per minute.

The Geminids

These appear during the second week of December, peaking on the 14th with about one per minute. Look towards the constellation of Gemini.

BUILD YOUR OWN SOLAR SYSTEM!

To get an idea of how big our galaxy is, you first need to understand how big our solar system is. The best way of doing that is to build a model of it.

Here's what you will need:
- Two small ball bearings
- Two peas
- A snooker ball
- A tennis ball
- Two golf or table tennis balls
- Two pinheads
- Some sand
- A washing machine

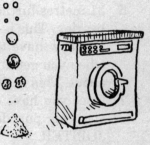

(If you are clever enough to understand this sort of thing, the scale of this model is going to be about 1:2,500,000.)

Here's the bad news – you are going to need a room about 2½ km long!

What you do:
1 Paint the washing machine yellow and put it at one end of the room. This is the SUN.
2 23 metres away from the SUN put down one of your ball bearings. This is MERCURY.
3 Keep going another 20 metres and then put down a pea. This is VENUS.
4 After a further 17 metres put down the other pea. This is EARTH. If you want to show the MOON,

49

put one of the pinheads down about 15 centimetres from the Earth.

5   31 metres further along put down the other ball bearing. This is MARS.
6   You now have to walk another 220 metres, but when you get about halfway sprinkle some sand about. This is the ASTEROID BELT.
7   Once you have completed your 220 metre walk you can put down the tennis ball, which is JUPITER.

8   260 metres later you can put down the snooker ball to represent SATURN.
9   Keep going for 577 metres ... then put down a golf ball. This is URANUS.
10 You'll have to go another 651 metres before you can put down the second golf ball, and this is NEPTUNE.

11 Your last distance is 561 metres, and you can finally put down your last pinhead. This is PLUTO.

There! You have made a rough scale model of the solar system with everything approximately the right size. Don't the planets look tiny in all that empty space? It makes you realize how clever scientists must be to send rockets out to visit them, and don't forget, the planets are not in a nice straight line but they all move round all the time!

So much for our planets, but just suppose we wanted to show the nearest star to our Sun on this model?

The star that comes nearest to us is called Proxima Centauri. Guess how far you would have to walk to fit in with the rest of your solar system model?

● 1,200 metres?
● 23 kilometres?
● 92 kilometres?
● 753 kilometres?
● 1,089 kilometres?
● The other side of the world?

While you are thinking about that, let's be sensible. As it is difficult to find a room long enough for our accurate solar system model, here's a smaller version you can make. The planets will not be the right sizes but the distances between them will be fairly accurate.

- You will need 10 of those nice drawing pins that have little round plastic heads and a piece of wood or card 600 millimetres long.
- Stick the first pin at the very end to represent the Sun. Measure off the other distances as shown in the diagram, and stick a pin in each place.

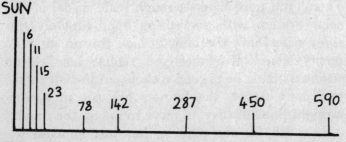

This model shows you how the planets are spaced in our solar system. The distances are all in millimetres.
- The nearest four to the Sun (Mercury, Venus, Earth and Mars) are known as the inner planets, and the others are the outer planets.

If you wanted to put our nearest star, Proxima Centauri, on this model, you would need to stick a pin in about 4 KILOmetres away!

As for the first model of the solar system, you would need to walk 16,856 kilometres to fit Proxima Centauri onto the model ... about the same distance as from Britain to Australia!

Planet sizes

This picture shows how big the planets are compared to each other. The four big ones are called the giants.

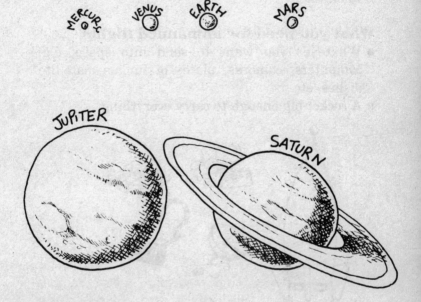

SPACE TRAVEL

There are two types of space travel: UNMANNED flights and MANNED flights. (Of course manned flights don't just have men on them, they have women too.)

What you need for unmanned flights
- Whatever you want to send into space, e.g. computers, cameras, plates of fungus, satellite dishes, etc.
- A rocket big enough to carry everything.

What you need for manned flights
- Pressurized living area for astronauts.
- A massive set of control panels for astronauts to work.
- Food supply.
- Air/water supply and waste processor.
- Heating and lighting.
- Whatever you want to send into space, e.g. computers, cameras, plates of fungus, satellite dishes, etc.

- If you want to land on somewhere else in space you need posh landing gear, maybe a buggy to drive round in, a big flag, golf clubs, and some way of taking off again.
- For return to Earth you need a suitable re-entry capsule, parachute or other necessary stuff to make sure astronauts land back safely.
- A rocket big enough to carry everything.

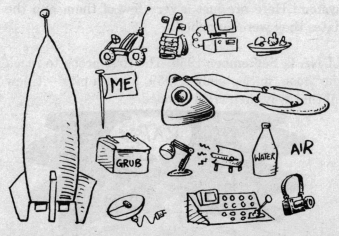

As you can see, there are two big problems about sending people up in rockets.

1 You have to keep them alive while they are up there.

2 You have to bring them back.

Astronauts insist on both of these before they go and they can get quite touchy if you suggest they are just being fussy.

What is a space probe?

If you are a doctor you might stick a probe in somebody to see what's going on. (Little children quite often probe their noses with their fingers and have to be told to stop it.) A space probe is very similar, we're just sticking a rocket up in the sky to see what we can find.

Some famous unmanned flights

Usually unmanned flights don't even come back to Earth and some have gone on right out of the solar system! Here are just a very few of them and the dates they were launched:

LUNA 2, September 1959. The first probe to reach the Moon, in September 1959. What a pity – it flew all that way then crash-landed.

VENERA 4, June 1967. The first probe to land on Venus AND send back data to tell us about it (in October 1967).

ZOND 5, September 1968. The first probe to go round the Moon and get back to Earth. It also had some very odd passengers – tortoises!

LUNA 16, September 1970. The first space souvenir hunter. It landed on the Moon, picked up a tiny bit of Moon rock and dust, then brought it back!

MARS 2 and 3, May 1971. The first probes to land on Mars but they only managed to send back a few seconds of data (in December 1971).

PIONEER 10, March 1972. First probe to reach Jupiter (in December 1973).

PIONEER 11, April 1973. First probe to reach Saturn (in September 1979).

MARINER 10, November 1973. First probe to reach Mercury (in March 1974).

VIKING 1, August 1975. The first really successful probe to land on Mars (in June 1976), it sent back information for 7 years!

GALILEO, October 1989. The first probe to try and land on Jupiter (in December 1995). It sent data back for nearly an hour before it got squashed, zapped and frazzled to bits.

OKAY— I KNOW WHEN I'M NOT WANTED.

...and the best probe yet!

VOYAGER 2, August 1977. It hopped past Jupiter and Saturn and after 8½ years of continuous flying it became the first probe to reach Uranus (in January 1986), then 3½ years later reached Neptune (in August 1989). Not only had it taken 12 years to reach Neptune but it was within 6 minutes of its expected arrival time! By the time it reached Neptune, Voyager 2's on-board equipment was 12 years out of date and it had spent 11 of those years only operating on its back-up receiver! However it discovered 10 more moons round Uranus, 6 more moons round Neptune and sent back some fabulous photographs. Voyager 2 has now left the solar system and is probably trying to send back the most amazing pictures on its tiny little wireless set. Unfortunately the signals are far too feeble for us to pick up and we've lost track of it.

Of course, they are still sending probes up which can go further and send back more detailed information, but it is unlikely that any of them will ever discover as many new things or delight the world as much as Voyager 2 did.

Not all unmanned space craft go to visit other planets. A lot of them just go up to put satellites in orbit, and one of the coolest things we've ever sent up has to be…

The Hubble Space Telescope

Even with the biggest telescopes on Earth you can never get a really clear picture because the Earth's atmosphere distorts what you see. The Hubble Space Telescope (or "HST" as groovy scientists call it) was sent up in 1990 and as there is no atmosphere to get in the way, it sends back pictures with 100 times more detail.

When it first went up there was a bit of a problem! The main component of the telescope was a very special curved mirror 2.4 metres across and it was not quite the right shape – it was about the width of a hair wrong! This resulted in one of the cleverest space missions yet. In December 1993 some astronauts went up in the Space Shuttle *Endeavour* and fixed an extra gadget into the HST to correct it. This mission took 11 days and involved 5 space walks and a LOT of nerve!

So much for unmanned flights, but now it's time we got into space ourselves.

Before humans went up into space, all sorts of animals including mice, dogs and monkeys were sent up to see if they could survive the trip.

There is a story that one monkey called Beezer actually made 5 space trips, and on the last trip a man was finally allowed to accompany him. Once the rocket had reached its parking orbit, both the man and Beezer had envelopes to open.

Beezer opened his envelope and his instructions read "Check height, altitude, speed and update geospace position on computer gyroscope. Ensure cabin life-support system is registering correct temperature and pressure, and check air recycling unit is functioning. Monitor fuel consumption and check computer wave link to Earth base is open on all channels."

The man opened his envelope and read his instructions: "Don't forget to feed the monkey."

Manned space flights

So far humans have only made little local excursions to the Moon or to space stations, mainly because they insist on coming home afterwards. However, suppose you wanted to do some serious space-hopping yourself...

● We'll have to assume that you have a rocket with plenty of food and water and you don't care if you come back or not!

● Before you set off you had better realize that trekking across space is not quite the same as getting the bus across town to visit your granny...

How to fly round space

By now you will have realized that space is pretty big. The only thing that is anywhere near us at all is the Moon, which is 384,000 km away.

If you were driving to the Moon in a car, you might need 25,000 litres of petrol to get there and another 25,000 litres to get back again. Obviously, in space there are no service stations, so you would have to take all your fuel with you.

HEY – WE'VE NEARLY ENOUGH TOKENS FOR A PLASTIC GOBLET!

PETROL

Even if you just wanted to drive over to the nearest planet, Venus, you would need to take millions of litres of fuel – enough to fill several swimming pools!

Of course, the more fuel you have to take with you, the heavier your car will be to start with. This means you need EVEN MORE fuel just to carry your extra fuel ... in fact the more fuel you take, the more you need! Luckily space travel is very different from riding in a car down a motorway. The hardest part about space travel is that you will use up most of your fuel in the first few minutes of your journey just blasting off from Earth. Why is it so hard to blast away from Earth? Because of...

Gravity

Every object in the universe (including you, this book and even drops of water) is surrounded by its own gravitational field which pulls other objects towards it.

I CAN'T HELP IT, IT'S BEING ATTRACTED TO MY GRAVITATIONAL FIELD!

The bigger an object is, the stronger its gravitational field. The planets all orbit the Sun because the Sun's gravity is so strong it can attract things millions of kilometres away. The Moon orbits the Earth because they pull on each other with their gravities. The reason the sea has tides is because the water is being pulled about by the gravities of the Sun and the Moon. Of course, even you are being affected by gravity because the Earth is pulling you towards it with its massive gravitational field – but at the same time YOU are pulling the EARTH towards you with your comparatively tiny gravitational field!

What is really spooky is that if you stand close to anyone (even somebody horrid), you will be attracted to each other by your gravity fields – but don't worry. The gravitational force between two people is less than the breeze from a gnat's wing.

There's one more very important thing about gravity: the further apart two objects are, the less the attraction between them. Thank goodness! Otherwise we'd never get into space at all.

Right then, so far you've got in your rocket and blasted away lots of fuel and now you find yourself moving up and away from Earth. The further away you move, the less you are affected by the Earth's gravity and eventually you will be able to "float" without using your engines at all.

Two other things make space travel easier:
● There is hardly anything to slow your rocket down

(no hills, no road friction, no traffic cones, and no air resistance), so it will glide on for ages without losing speed. You only need to use the engines very occasionally for steering.

● As you head across the solar system, you can use the gravitational fields of other planets to give your rocket a "boost".

Oddly enough, although gravity does its best to stop you setting off from Earth, once you are up in space it is very good at helping you to shoot off in the right direction ... but enough talk. There's only one way to really find out about all this.

Let's go for a test drive!

Get into your rocket then, and as well as having enough fuel, make sure you've got enough to eat and drink because this is going to be a long trip.

Three ... two ... one ... BLAST OFF!

● You feel like a rhinoceros has just rammed into your back as the rocket accelerates up into the sky. If you suddenly get an itchy nose ... tough luck! When you try to lift your hand from your armrest to scratch it, you won't be able to because your arm feels like it weighs a ton.

Wooo!

- Gradually the acceleration decreases and you feel less like an elephant is sitting on your lap.
- Before long you might hear a couple of little bangs and maybe some clunking noises. This means your rocket has used up all the fuel in your booster tanks, and so your computer has fired the explosive bolts to throw them away. (The empty tanks are useless now so you don't want to be heaving them all the way round space, do you?)

Parking in space

A few thousand miles up everything gets quieter because your motors shut down. You have reached a "parking" orbit. This means the rocket is travelling round Earth in a big circle at just the right height and the right speed so that it does not get any higher or any lower. Because there is no atmosphere there is nothing to slow you down, so you don't need the engines.

Time to relax as we do a few laps of our mother planet. Undo your seat belt and wait for it ... float about! Yes, you are now weightless, but don't spin yourself around too much until you get used to it. The effect on your stomach is ten times worse than the meanest roller coaster! You don't want to spend the rest of your journey cleaning sick off the control panel.

We've got a few hours in this parking orbit before we cruise on into space, so let's see how an orbit works.

Suppose you are flying above a planet such as the Earth...

If you suddenly stop you will fall to the ground – SCHPLATT!

If you go too slowly you will gradually come down – and if you haven't got your landing gear ready – KERUNCH!

If you are going too fast, the gravity of the planet might deflect you a bit, but you will shoot off into space – ZOOM!

But if you are going at exactly the right speed, you will find yourself orbiting the planet – WHEE!

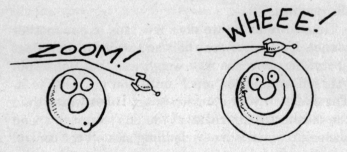

The right speed for orbiting depends on how high up you are ... the further out your orbit is from Earth, the slower you have to go.

One example of an orbit: If you are 36,000 km above the Earth you need to travel at 11,000 km/h. This particular orbit is very important because you will be travelling around the Earth once every 24 hours. Of course this is how long it takes the Earth to spin round, so if you are going the right way you will always be above the same place on the ground. (This orbit is called "geosynchronous".) Many satellites orbit at this height including the one which transmits satellite TV stations!

Of course it isn't just rockets than do orbits. Our Moon is orbiting the Earth at a height of 384,000 km, and Earth is orbiting the Sun at a height of 150 million km...

Right then, now we know about orbits it's time to move on. One little thrust on our engines is enough to speed us up, this breaks us out of our parking orbit and so we find ourselves zooming out into space. Of course, the real knack of space travel is to leave the orbit at exactly the right time, to the nearest fraction of a second. That way we launch ourselves as accurately as possible at our next destination and so we will use less fuel correcting our course along the way.

Getting a boost, or Cosmic pinball and Scottish country dancing

Although we can travel millions of miles through space hardly using the engines, we do need to take the opportunity of a free boost if we can get it. The main way of doing this is called the "gravity assist" technique, which is a bit like playing a giant cosmic pinball table.

To understand how this works, you need a very sympathetic friend called Morag and a bit of clear floorspace. A tape of some Scottish dance music (such as Wee Jimmy MacSporran and his Hot Haggis Band) might help but this is not absolutely vital. Here's what to do:

1 Get Morag to dance round you in a big circle keeping about 5 metres away.

2 Put on the tape if you have one.

3 Skip lightly towards Morag with your arm outstretched.

4 As you pass Morag, get her to grab your arm and swing you round a quarter turn and then let go.

5 Unless Morag is particularly weedy, you will probably end up flying head first into the nearest wall.

Silly as this seems, you can do the same with rockets and planets providing you pick a time when everything is in the right place.

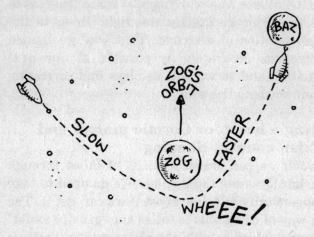

Here you want to get to planet BAZ but you are going too slowly. Luckily planet ZOG has a nice strong gravitational field and is in a good position to help. Basically you are going to grab hold of ZOG as it goes past, pick up speed then let go!

If you like you can put on your tape of Wee Jimmy MacSporran as your rocket cruises gently up to ZOG.

Concentrate, because your aim here is absolutely crucial. You need to calculate your exact speed and then work out exactly how close to ZOG you need to approach.

- If you get too close you will crash, just as if you ran straight into Morag and knocked her over.
- If you don't get close enough Zog's gravity will not be able to catch you and you will go limping off into empty space. This is the same as if you didn't get close enough to Morag for her to grab your arm.
- BUT ... if you get it just right Zog's gravity will catch you and swing you round just like Morag did and you will be thrown towards BAZ.

So far, then, you've got the hang of launching into space, parking in space and powering your way across space. The only other thing you need to learn about is...

Landing
The most important thing here is you must be very careful where you choose to land.

- If you land on a planet or moon with too much gravity you will not be able to get off again. (Remember: taking off uses masses of fuel and you haven't brought very much with you.)
- You must ensure the landing surface is what your

69

rocket is designed for. You may need it to be solid ground or you might prefer it to be liquid such as a big ocean.

So far humans have only visited the Moon, which has a solid surface, and luckily the gravity is quite weak so they could come back again. With current technology it is very hard to imagine how humans could visit anywhere else without getting stuck.

Of course most rocket landings have been done by people coming back to Earth.

What used to happen is that when a rocket got back from space, it orbited Earth a few times (to help line up where it was going to come down), then it would plummet through the atmosphere getting extremely hot in the process, and finally a capsule with the astronauts in it would land by parachute and splash in the sea. Although this worked quite well it meant each rocket could only be used once.

More recently, the Space Shuttle was designed to come in to land rather like an aeroplane. This is much better because even though during the course of its flight it will have thrown away empty fuel tanks, the most expensive parts of the rocket remain intact and can be used again.

In a perfect world they would have a launch

system which didn't need tons of fuel, and rockets wouldn't be littering the sky up with empty fuel tanks. Here's one idea:

JUST CLIMB THE 50 MILLION STEPS AND YOU'll FIND THE ROCKET AT THE TOP.

Now you've had your driving lesson, let's have some fun!

LET'S POP IN ON THE NEIGHBOURS

We are going to visit all the other planets in our solar system and find out all about the weird things that make these other worlds different from our own BUT ... before we go, we must plan the journey! (Space is extremely big and planets are terribly tiny, so we could very easily get lost if we don't!)

In our solar system we have nine planets to visit. Wouldn't it be handy if they were all in a straight line so we could just visit them one by one, travelling the shortest distance between them?

THAT WAS EASY —
NOW HOME FOR TEA!

Unfortunately they all orbit round the Sun at different speeds so they are far more likely to be laid out all over the place like this:

START
HERE!

Mind you, it wouldn't be any help to us if the planets were in a straight line because with current technology we have to rely on the "gravity assist" technique to keep our rocket up to a decent speed. (Does 100,000 km/h seem fast enough for you?) This means the planets need to be in a CURVED line. A possible route round a few of them would have to look more like this:

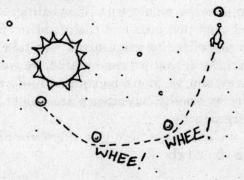

Of course this takes a LOT of planning. An even bigger problem is that if we wanted to see ALL the planets, they are only likely to be conveniently positioned like this once in several thousand years.

We will have to assume that:
- We have a super advanced rocket that can go any distance at any speed without using gravity assist techniques.
- Our rocket is SO super and advanced that it can land anywhere and take off again, even if the local gravity is very strong.
- The planets are neatly laid out in a line with the minimum distance between them, and they won't move out of the way before we get there.

73

There is just one very final thing to consider before we go...

Will the other planets be safe?

Although humans have only travelled as far as the Moon, space probes have been much further and sent back details of what we can expect and how dangerous different places are likely to be.

Visiting another planet isn't like visiting another town. You can't just land and then toddle off to see if there's anywhere to get a drink. We take it for granted on Earth that we can breathe, we won't get blown away and we won't be squished into a pancake shape by gravity, but other places might not be quite so friendly.

Before we land anywhere else there are SEVEN things we should check:

PLANET CHECK LIST:
1. PLANET SURFACE
2. GRAVITY STRENGTH
3 ATMOSPHERE
4. PRESSURE (ATMOSPHERIC)
5. TEMPERATURE
6. RADIATION LEVEL
7 WIND STRENGTH

Suppose an alien came to Earth, here's how this list might look:

PLANET CHECK LIST:

1. PLANET SURFACE — NEARLY 3/4 IS COVERED IN A HARMLESS, NON-CORROSIVE LIQUID, THE REST IS MOSTLY SAFE AND SOLID.

2. GRAVITY STRENGTH — MEDIUM. ENOUGH TO HOLD YOU DOWN WITHOUT SQUASHING YOU.

3. ATMOSPHERE — MEDIUM. NITROGEN/OXYGEN MIXTURE, CAN SUPPORT LIFE WITHOUT BEING DANGEROUS.*

4. PRESSURE — MEDIUM. ENOUGH TO STOP YOU EXPLODING, BUT NOT SO MUCH TO MAKE YOU IMPLODE.

5. TEMPERATURE — MEDIUM. NOT COLD ENOUGH TO FREEZE GAS, OR HOT ENOUGH TO MELT METAL.*

6. RADIATION — MINIMUM LEVELS GENERALLY HARMLESS.*

7. WIND — HARDLY ANY. 150 KM/H GUSTS OF WIND ARE VERY RARE.

Sadly, a clever alien might feel some details need an extra note, like this:

*Radiation, Temperature and Atmosphere have been safe for many millions of years but so-called "intelligent" Earth life-forms are very close to upsetting all these. At present the atmosphere is close to breakdown, and in turn this could cause the temperature to shoot up. Artificially produced radiation is also close to getting out of control.

The essential atmosphere

Most of the things on the check list are fairly obvious, but you may be wondering why having an atmosphere is so important – in fact if the atmosphere is poisonous like it is on most planets, it's useless to you anyway, isn't it? Not really, because without any atmosphere at all...

● You would be more likely to get hit by a meteorite.
● You might get zapped by space radiation.
● You would explode.
● Your blood would boil and evaporate.

An atmosphere burns up all but the biggest meteorites before they can do any damage and it also acts as a radiation shield. Mind you, there won't be any time to worry about this because you will already have exploded and your blood will have boiled away! This is because without an atmosphere, there isn't any atmospheric pressure.

Why do we need atmospheric pressure?

Have you ever been to the bottom of a deep swimming pool? If so you will have felt the water pushing in at you: you'll particularly feel it in your chest. This is because if you are 2 metres deep, effectively you are under a pile of water 2 metres high and that weighs quite a lot! If you go much deeper you need special equipment to stop the weight of the water squashing you to a pulp. There are some creatures that live at the very bottom of the ocean which have adapted to cope with the very high pressure, but their trouble is that they can't cope with lower pressure. If you bring one up to the surface, because there's not enough pressing against them, they explode!

As you stand on the surface of Earth above you is more than 80 km of air. Now you might not think air weighs very much, but 80 km of it adds up and the weight of this air pushing down creates what we call atmospheric pressure. If the atmospheric pressure disappeared, the same thing would happen to us as the deep ocean creature. We would all burst open like balloons full of purple slime. SHPLITCH!

The atmospheric pressure also controls what temperatures liquids boil at. If the pressure gets very low then any liquid will start boiling, including your blood!

The black sky warning
On Earth in daytime the sky is blue because of the way the sunlight shines through our atmosphere. Here's a useful check: if you're on a planet and can see the Sun but the sky is black then BEWARE – there is no atmosphere.

Strange years and days

You probably know that Earth is flying round the Sun in a big circle and to get right round once takes a year. As well as flying round the Sun, Earth spins like a top and to spin round one time takes a day. On Earth our days are a lot shorter than years, in fact the Earth spins round about 365 times for each trip right round the Sun. That's why we have 365 days in most years. On other planets you will find years and days can be very different.

By now you will be itching to go so let's BLAST OFF!

To begin with we are going to pass by Venus and (if the planets are in their nice convenient straight line) after about 90 million km we will reach the little planet nearest the Sun, which is:

MERCURY

Every planet has its own sign.
This is Mercury's.

PLANET CHECK LIST:

1. **PLANET SURFACE**   SOLID ROCK AND CRATERS.

2. **GRAVITY STRENGTH**   WEAK (LESS THAN $\frac{1}{2}$ OF EARTH'S).

3. **ATMOSPHERE**   HELIUM, SODIUM POTASSIUM.

4. **PRESSURE**   ALMOST NONE.

5. **TEMPERATURE**   MASSIVE RANGE FROM $-180°$ TO $+430°$.

6. **RADIATION**   BEWARE! INTENSE RADIATION FROM SUN.

7. **WIND**   NONE.

We can check the list and see that Mercury is nice and solid to land on.

- Gravity is weak which means we can jump 4 metres high if we like.
- The changes in temperature are a big problem – sometimes it is hot enough to make rocks glow and other times it would freeze the beak off a penguin. You simply wouldn't know what to wear.
- The pressure is dangerously low, but in some ways that is GOOD NEWS because the atmosphere itself is pretty nasty. Helium is completely useless to breathe, and chemicals like

79

sodium and potassium in the air would be like breathing acid!

- Even if you could survive everything else, you'd get zapped to death on Mercury because the Sun gets very close and it kicks out lethal radiation by the truckload.

Ignoring such trifles as instant death, the big question arises...

What's worth doing on Mercury?

It sounds a bit weedy, but the grooviest experience on Mercury is to watch the Sun, which does two things that we NEVER see on Earth.

- It gets bigger and smaller.
- It seems to go forwards AND backwards.

On Earth we're used to the Sun being rather boring. All we ever see is this:

- The Sun comes up one side.
- The Sun goes down the other side.

In summer the Sun takes longer about it and also reaches a higher point in the sky but otherwise every day is pretty much the same.

On Mercury it's far more interesting. Here's what you might see:

- The Sun appears over the horizon.
- As well as moving up in the sky, the Sun gets bigger.
- When the Sun is high overhead it stops, then starts to slip back down the way it came!
- The Sun changes its mind AGAIN and continues across the sky.
- It gets smaller as it approaches the horizon.

- Just before it sets, the Sun decides to come back up again.
- Finally it decides to finish its journey and disappears below the horizon.

The bigger and smaller bit is easy to understand. Most of the planets go round the Sun in a circle, but Mercury actually goes round in an ellipse shape, which means that sometimes it gets closer to the Sun than others.

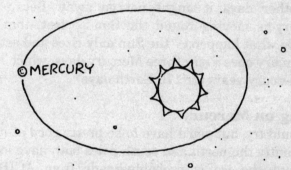

Of course, when Mercury is close to the Sun, the Sun looks bigger than when it is far away. (At its biggest the Sun looks three times wider than it does from Earth.) The distance between Mercury and the Sun varies from 46 million km to 70 million km.

So how does the Sun seem to move backwards? Oddly enough, this is due to the fact that there are only 1½ Mercury days in a Mercury year. It only takes Mercury 88 days to move right round the Sun because it hasn't nearly as far to go as Earth and it moves three times as fast. Mercury also spins round like Earth does but much slower – in fact it takes about 59 Earth days to spin round once. This means

81

that a Mercury year is as long as 88 Earth days and a Mercury day is as long as 59 Earth days. Simple, eh?

We get a sunrise every day because every time Earth spins round we see the Sun come up. That's because the Earth hasn't moved very far round the Sun and so as far as we're concerned the Sun is pretty much in the same place. However, suppose the Sun wasn't always in the same place, that would mean that some days the Sun might not come up, and other days it might not go away. Because Mercury is moving round the Sun so fast, that's roughly what happens – the Sun only rises and sets on Mercury once every three Mercury days, which is two Mercury years (or 176 Earth days).

Skiing on Mercury

You could try, but you'd have to be pretty good at it. Apparently the north and south poles both have ice caps but the ice is probably made from ACID. Unless you were really fast it would melt your skis, boots, expensive skiing trousers and matching gloves. In fact all that might be left of you is your bobble hat, which is too naff even for acid space ice to stomach.

SIZZLE!

What would a Mercurian look like?

Sadly there aren't any aliens on Mercury (or any-where else we know about for that matter) but just suppose some sort of creature had evolved, what could you expect?

Because gravity is so low the Mercurian would be able to grow very tall, maybe as high as a five-storey building. To give it a chance against the change in temperatures, all the delicate inside bits would be kept in a sort of vacuum flask. The outside would be shiny silver to reflect the heat from the Sun and any eyes would be able to shut right down to tiny little dots for when the Sun is bright, and then open up like umbrellas for when it gets dark.

Good conversation lines might be:

"Argh! My trousers have caught fire."

"Brr, my eyeballs have frozen over." (Repeat these every few hours.)

"I think my sundial needs mending."

"Look, isn't that a bobble hat on that ice cap?"

So much for Mercury. Turn round because we are now going to head out away from the Sun. If our planets are still conveniently in line, it will only be about 50 million km to our next stop, so let's blast off and check out...

VENUS ♀

PLANET CHECK LIST:

1. **PLANET SURFACE** — SOLID ROCK, CRATERS AND MASSIVE VOLCANOES.

2. **GRAVITY STRENGTH** — NEARLY AS STRONG AS EARTH'S.

3. **ATMOSPHERE** — CARBON DIOXIDE WITH HIGH CLOUDS OF SULPHURIC ACID.

4. **PRESSURE** — MASSIVE – NEARLY 100 TIMES MORE THAN EARTH.

5. **TEMPERATURE** — EXACTLY 459° ALL OVER.

6. **RADIATION** — NOT A PROBLEM.

7. **WIND** — NONE AT GROUND LEVEL BUT ACID CLOUDS MOVE AT 360 KM/H.

Venus looks gorgeous as you approach it. It's pink and shiny and looks like a great place to visit but DON'T BE FOOLED.

● If the high speed ACID clouds don't dissolve you and your rocket, then as you get close to the surface you are probably going to burn up because

the temperature is hot enough to melt lead.
- If you do manage to land ... DO NOT STEP OUT OF YOUR ROCKET. The atmospheric pressure will squash you into a little jelly.

If you do decide to risk a look round you'll see lots of rocks and craters glowing in the heat, and the cloudy sky is orange. There are a couple of volcanoes called Rhea and Theia which are much more massive than anything we have on Earth. Although they seem quite sleepy, we can't be absolutely sure that they don't still go off occasionally. By now you will have realized that Venus is a pretty nasty place to be – you could end up being a dissolved, burnt jelly covered in molten lava!

WHAT A WELCOME!

You may be wondering why Venus is so hot – after all, it's even hotter than Mercury although it's twice as far away from the Sun. The reason is the carbon dioxide atmosphere. This lets in all the heat from the Sun but doesn't let it out again.

When people on Earth talk about the "greenhouse effect", they are worrying about the growing amount of carbon dioxide in our air. The problem is that cars and factories make carbon dioxide and we're building more and more of them. Trees and plants get rid of carbon dioxide but we keep getting rid of them. If carbon dioxide levels get too high then we might eventually get as hot as Venus!

Strange days

Venus has one particularly odd feature. It takes Venus about 225 Earth days to go round the Sun, and it takes 243 Earth days to spin round once. This means the Venus day is longer than the Venus year! It also spins backwards compared to the other planets.

How to make a model of a planet spinning backwards

Get something soft and round like an orange, and stick a pencil or something right through the middle. Where the pencil goes into your "Planet" is the North Pole and where it comes out is the South Pole.

MERCURY　　EARTH　　VENUS

Hold the pencil straight up and start your planet turning from left to right. There, you've made a model of how Mercury spins. Keep the planet turning and tip your pencil over a bit. Now you've got a model of how Earth spins. Now keep your planet turning the same way but tip your pencil right over until it is upside down. That's how Venus spins … the wrong way round!

The Venus creature

If a creature evolved on Venus, it would have to be very small and round to help it cope with the immense atmospheric pressure – so it might look a bit like a tortoise. Most of what it would be saying is "ouch, ooyah, eek" as it kept stepping on the smouldering rocks. Because Venus is such a hot, dangerous place it would be trying to sell you either a fridge or life insurance.

How to make friends on Venus

Take a normal kitchen oven and turn it on full. People would be queuing to get in it – just to cool off! If you offered them an ice-cream they would probably make you their president.

Time to get off Venus, and if we're lucky we should only have about 40 million km to go before we reach the third planet from the Sun. Does it look familiar? It should because we've got back to...

EARTH

Things you can do on Earth that you can't do anywhere else

- Buy chips.
- Watch telly.
- Run around outside for more than a second without any clothes on (even if you do get some funny looks).

Earth is altogether a pretty nice place, but you know that already so we won't spend too long here. However, there is one thing in particular that Earth has got that Mercury and Venus haven't. Earth has got a natural satellite which we call:

THE MOON

It's only about 380,000 km from Earth (or as we used to say "a quarter of a million miles"), so let's drop in as we're passing.

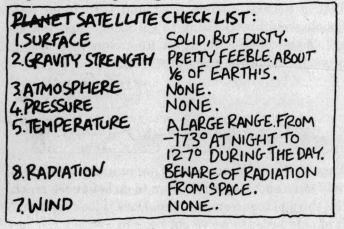

PLANET SATELLITE CHECK LIST:
1. SURFACE — SOLID, BUT DUSTY.
2. GRAVITY STRENGTH — PRETTY FEEBLE. ABOUT ⅙ OF EARTH'S.
3. ATMOSPHERE — NONE.
4. PRESSURE — NONE.
5. TEMPERATURE — A LARGE RANGE. FROM −173° AT NIGHT TO 127° DURING THE DAY.
8. RADIATION — BEWARE OF RADIATION FROM SPACE.
7. WIND — NONE.

WHY CAN'T YOU HAVE A GOOD PARTY ON THE MOON?

BECAUSE THERE'S NO ATMOSPHERE!

Being on the Moon is very like being on Mercury, although happily it doesn't get nearly so hot and the radiation isn't quite such a problem.

Moon days and nights

Because the Moon stays with Earth as it goes round the Sun, the Moon "year" is the same as Earth's. What is more important is that the Moon itself is going round Earth, and it takes 27 days, 7 hours and 43 minutes to do this. The Moon is also spinning round, and guess what? To spin round once takes 27 days, 7 hours and 43 minutes ... it's exactly the same. This means that from Earth we always see the same side of the Moon, and in fact we never saw the other side until we sent rockets up there.

Imagine you're sitting in a swivel chair in the middle of a room and somebody called Janet is walking round and round you, but always facing you. Obviously if you swivel round and watch her, you will always see her face. Janet is acting just like the Moon in that she is spinning herself round once every time she goes round you.

JANET SLOWLY TURNS TO STAY FACING YOU.

YOU SWIVEL.

Suppose the Moon didn't spin at all when it went round the Earth, that would be the same as Janet walking round you, but always facing the same corner of the room. Sometimes you would see the back of her head, and other times you would see her face.

JANET FACES ONE WAY ONLY.

YOU SWIVEL.

Thank you, Janet, for making this book a fuller experience for us all.

Looking home...

If you were on the Moon and looking at Earth, you would find that Earth would always be in exactly the same place in the sky, and it would be spinning round – so if you started looking at Australia, 12 hours later you would be seeing Europe. You would also see Earth go through different phases like the Moon does – sometimes you would only see a crescent shape and other times you would see a complete round Earth.

Moon time

On the Moon the Sun would still come up and go down, but you would find that one complete Moon day and night would be 30 Earth days long. If you went to live on the Moon and took your watch with you, you'd find it was over 700 hours between one "midnight" and the next. This means that you could have times like twenty past four hundred and nine, or quarter to six hundred and four or even "it's exactly one hundred and thirty-five o'clock". If you had a cuckoo clock it would probably blow up.

90

What to do on the Moon

Take your bucket and spade because one of the most satisfying pastimes is to build sandcastles ... or to be more precise moondust castles. This is because the Moon has no atmosphere so there can't be any wind and your castles will be there for ever. While you're up there, look out for the footprints left by the first astronauts who visited the Moon in 1969 – they will still be there, too.

The Moonoids

If creatures evolved on the Moon they would be even taller than the ones on Mercury. They would have fur coats to keep the chill out and lots of arms carrying feather dusters and vacuum cleaner attachments because everything is so dusty. As Moon days and nights are so long they would have massive bags under their eyes, and for fun they would ride about on space kangaroos which could jump massive distances.

A soppy thing to say on the Moon:

OOH HOW ROMANTIC, THERE'S A FULL EARTH OUT TONIGHT.

If we pick our time right, our next destination will be just under 80 million km away, so let's cruise casually on to the fourth planet from the Sun, which is:

MARS

PLANET CHECK LIST:

1. **PLANET SURFACE** ROCKY MOUNTAINS, DEEP CHASMS. MASSIVE VOLCANOES.

2. **GRAVITY STRENGTH** WEAK (LESS THAN ½ EARTH'S).

3. **ATMOSPHERE** MAINLY CARBON DIOXIDE.

4. **PRESSURE** PATHETIC (LESS THAN 1% OF EARTH'S).

5. **TEMPERATURE** BETWEEN -130° TO -30° BUT CAN REACH 17° IN SUMMER.

6. **RADIATION** SOME THREAT FROM SPACE RADIATION.

7. **WIND** GENERALLY WEAK, BUT SOME DUST STORMS.

Here you'll find some very chilly nights and low pressure, but otherwise Mars isn't such a dangerous place to visit. It's certainly no worse than the Moon, providing you find a clear landing site.

Mars is known as the Red Planet, so don't be too shocked to find that the rocky landscape is red. There are some awesome volcanoes, including Olympus Mons which is three times bigger than Earth's Mount Everest! Luckily none of them seem to be erupting any more.

Skiing on Mars

YES! YES! YES! Mars must be the ultimate ski resort. It's got loads of big icy mountains and craters to go whizzing down, and to make your holiday photos a bit more spectacular some of the ice is frozen carbon dioxide. This is the same stuff that pop groups use to give big smoke effects on the stage. If you go skiing down it you'll have a brilliant trail of white smoke shooting out from under your skis.

Years and days

Of all the other planets, Martian years and days are the most similar to Earth's. A Martian year is 687 Earth days long which means one Martian year is a bit less than two of our Earth years. Days on Mars are 24 hours and 37 minutes long so they are just a bit longer than Earth. You could lie in bed an extra 37 minutes every morning and still not get up late.

Martian moons

On Earth we only have one natural satellite, the Moon, but Mars has two called Phobos and Deimos. You might be feeling jealous about this but don't be. Our moon is 3,500 km across and it has to be said that it is one of the biggest and prettiest in the solar system. Weedy little Phobos is only 27 km across and if you think that's pathetic, you'll laugh when you know that Deimos is only 15 km across. If you were standing on Mars Deimos would look about the size and shape of a potato at the far end of a football pitch, and about as interesting.

Is there life on Mars?

In fact, everybody had pretty much given up looking for life on Mars until recently when there was absolutely MASSIVE excitement. What had they found, eh? Green aliens buzzing round with plasma guns? Giant talking space trees? Intelligent cloning organisms that can assume any appearance? (Be careful – this book might be one.)

No, not quite. They were examining a meteorite that had landed 13,000 years ago near Earth's south pole and decided that it had originally come from Mars. In the meteorite they found some very tiny little shapes in the rock which they think are fossils – in other words shapes made by living things. These "Martians" died millions of years ago. They were probably some sort of simple plant, and a hundred of them could fit across the width of a single hair. Nevertheless everybody got really thrilled because if life could exist somewhere other than Earth, who knows? It could be all over the galaxy.

The Martian

Let's suppose the tiny thing that made the fossil had managed to evolve. As Mars is quite cold, it would live underground to keep warm so it would be a sort of mole with diamond teeth for crunching rock.

When it emerged on the surface it would need bigger eyes to help it see because sunlight will only be half as bright. It will have developed great big long feet to zoom down the icy slopes without hiring skis, and really groovy Martians might only have one foot to go snow boarding instead. Of course, being skiers they will come in an amazing range of tasteless colours and be wearing bobble hats.

Things to say to irritate Martians:
"Nice planet, shame about the moons."
"Are you SURE that volcano's safe?"
"Of course, you haven't REALLY skied until you've been to Mercury."

It's time to continue our journey and this is where things get serious. Instead of just pottering around the inner planets doing trips of 80 million km or so, we're going to have to cover some serious space if we're going to reach the GIANT PLANETS. The next planet we hope to visit is Jupiter which at best is over 550 million km from Mars. However, we can't just set the autopilot and relax because we're about to do the most dangerous part of the trip! We have to pass through...

THE ASTEROID BELT

Between Mars and Jupiter are thousands of asteroids which are all orbiting the Sun just like lots of tiny planets. The biggest is 1,000 km across and called Ceres, the smallest is smaller than a grain of sand and if anybody could find it they would probably call it Diddley Squit. If we hope to get from Mars to Jupiter in less than a year we'll have to travel at least 60,000 km per hour, and at that speed even hitting Diddley Squit could cause a lot of damage.

Asteroid facts
- Most asteroids are spinning round.
- Some asteroids are so similar to little planets that they even have their own mini moons going round them.
- Some asteroids don't care where they go – one or two have even come so close to Earth that they scared everybody.
- The asteroids probably resulted from a planet which tried to form during the early life of the solar system, but got pulled to bits by Jupiter's massive gravitational field.
- Bigger asteroids tend to be round but smaller ones can be all sorts of funny shapes. There's one called Eros which is a bit like a 37 km long sausage.

The Asteroid game!

All the deep space probes so far have managed to pass through the Asteroid Belt intact. This took a lot of skill but also a LOT of luck! Here's a game to see if you can get through the Asteroid Belt. To play you will need a normal six-sided dice. You might like to challenge a friend and take alternate turns.

- To start your trip through the asteroid belt you have to keep throwing the dice until you get a 1 then move into the "1" region.
- You then have to keep throwing until you get a 2, then keep throwing until you get a 3, then a 4 and then a 5 to move through the regions.
- Finally, keep throwing until you get a 6. If you suceed, then you have got through the asteroid belt!

This all seems very simple BUT...

If at any time you throw the same number as your last throw then YOU HAVE COLLIDED WITH AN ASTEROID! See what number is on the dice, then look at the chart to tell what has happened:

1 You hit an ant-sized asteroid which cracked your protection shield. Carry on, but if you hit any more asteroids, your rocket blows to bits.

2 You narrowly clipped a tiny asteroid that scratched your paint. Unless your protection shield is already cracked, keep playing.

3 You hit a pea-sized asteroid. You are very lucky not to blow up (as long as your protection shield is still OK), but you must start again.

4 You just brushed past Phaethon – an erratic 5 km wide asteroid – and you are sent spinning off. Throw the dice once more and whatever number comes up, continue from that region.

5 You hit Diddley Squit which dented your rocket and slowed you down. You must throw another five before continuing.

6 You collided with CERES and you are smashed into thousands of tiny pieces. Bye bye.

Did you survive the Asteroid Belt? If so, we'll zoom on to sample the delights of...

JUPITER

$$\boxed{4}$$

PLANET CHECK LIST:

1. PLANET SURFACE — NOTHING TO PITCH A TENT ON.

2. GRAVITY STRENGTH — A LOT MORE THAN EARTH.

3. ATMOSPHERE — MAINLY HYDROGEN WITH SOME HELIUM.

4. PRESSURE — INCREDIBLE.

5. TEMPERATURE — BETWEEN $-125°$ AND $+17°$.

6. RADIATION — ABSOLUTE KILLER!

7. WIND — STORMS AND WHIRL-WINDS TOO HORRENDOUS TO MEASURE.

This is the first of the GIANT PLANETS we've visited and if this wasn't a pretend journey, there's absolutely no doubt that it would be the last. Even 150,000 km away Jupiter's radiation is five hundred times the lethal dose: it's even enough to chew up the computer in your space rocket.

Jupiter the Fatty

The main thing to know about Jupiter is that it is by far the biggest planet in the solar system. It is 317 times heavier than Earth, and if you could put the other planets on a giant balance scale you'd find it is more than twice as heavy as all the other planets put together. What's so weird is that even though it is so heavy, most of Jupiter is just GAS. This might make you think that you're about to visit a big cloud ... wrong!

Because Jupiter is so big, it has a MASSIVE gravitational field which is so strong it squashes the planet into itself. Not only does this cause the gruesome radiation levels, but the gas at the centre of the planet turns into blue liquid and even a clear metal. This metal is solid hydrogen and if you know anything about chemistry, this will freak you out! On Earth in normal conditions, solid hydrogen has to be colder than MINUS 259°C which is only 14° above absolute zero – the coldest temperature possible. On Jupiter it doesn't need to be as cold as this, instead the hydrogen is made solid by the atmospheric pressure which quite frankly doesn't bear thinking about.

By now you will have realized that landing on Jupiter is a bit of a no-no, you're better off cruising above the atmosphere in a suit made out of lead plates 3m thick to protect you from the radiation. (You might look silly but at least you've got an excuse not to go jogging.)

What can you see on Jupiter?

● THE GIANT RED SPOT: This is the most famous thing on Jupiter. Don't worry, although it's thousands of miles across, it isn't infectious. The red spot is actually a massive storm like a super hurricane.

● MEGA LIGHTNING FLASHES: Hold your ears because there are thunderclaps to match! Jupiter has massive storms all the time.

● COSMIC CLOUDS: The upper atmosphere contains some ammonia which freezes and leads to some amazing colour schemes.

● DARK BELTS: Going round the middle of Jupiter are some strange dark "belts" caused by different formations in the clouds.

● A WONKY COMPASS: On Earth a compass always points north because Earth has a magnetic field – which is like having a big magnet running up through the centre. Your compass will work brilliantly on Jupiter because the magnetic field is 14 times stronger. Just one warning though ... Jupiter's magnetic field is upside down compared to Earth's so the compass needle will actually point at the south pole instead of the north.

Years and days on Jupiter

Jupiter takes nearly 12 of our years to go round the sun, which is fair enough because it has much further to go. However, the Jupiter day is really impressive: big fat Jupiter manages to spin round on itself once every 9 hours and 50 minutes. Because it spins so fast and it is made of gas this has a funny effect ... Jupiter bulges out at the sides!

It's a bit like a Scotsman doing a twirl in his kilt apart from the fact that Jupiter doesn't need to wear pants.

IF JUPITER DIDN'T SPIN

BUT BECAUSE IT SPINS QUICKLY!

This fast spinning is also one of the reasons why the dark bands form – some of the clouds can't keep up with the others.

Jupiter's moons

Jupiter has four big moons, and 12 smaller moons of various shapes and sizes.

Just in case anybody asks you, here's all their names starting with the closest one to the planet and moving outwards:
Metis, Adrastea, Amalthea, Thebe, Io, Europa, Ganymede, Callisto, Leda, Himalia, Lysithea, Earwax, Elara, Ananke, Carme, Pasiphaë, Sinope.
Just for fun, there's an extra name in the list which is too silly even for a Jupiter moon. Did you spot it?

If you have some good binoculars, you can see the four big moons from Earth and if you visited them you would find they are all very different.

IO is 3,642 km across and covered in active volcanoes. From Jupiter it looks slightly bigger than our moon does from Earth. (It's the only moon in the solar system that does appear bigger than ours from the nearest planet.) Photographs of Io look a bit like a pizza – but if you go there don't try it. It tastes horrible.

EUROPA is 3,130 km across and like a big dirty snooker ball. There are a few dark lines on it but no decent hills or craters.

GANYMEDE is 5,268 km across, which is bigger than the planet Mercury. Although it is the biggest moon in the solar system, from Jupiter it only looks half the size of Io because it's a lot further away. It is icy and has craters but no working volcanoes.

CALLISTO is 4,806 km across and again is icy with craters, but in particular it has two strange "basins" called Valhalla and Asgard. These are like massive dents in the surface about 300 km across and each is surrounded by a pattern of rings. Very odd.

The only weedy thing about Jupiter

Everybody knows that Saturn has a brilliant system of rings round it, and you'll find out all about them soon. What most people don't know is that Jupiter also has a ring system, but it is dark and feeble and if Saturn had anybody living on it, they'd be shouting rude things like "feeble", "pathetic", and "don't ring us, we'll ring you".

The Jovian

As Jupiter does not have any reasonable surface to land on, the Jupiter alien (or Jovian) will be like some massive hot air balloon so it can float above the planet all the time. There's no chance of finding

anything that we might recognize as food around Jupiter, so instead it will have learnt to survive on radiation that will make it glow, and which it collects with long wispy tendrils. Of course, as it doesn't eat it won't need a mouth.

What do you say to a Jovian?

Anything you like – it can't answer back. How about:

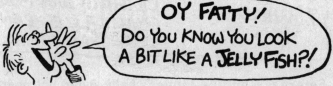

OY FATTY! DO YOU KNOW YOU LOOK A BIT LIKE A JELLY FISH?!

Actually, you'd better not risk being cheeky. Who knows, it might have a way of blasting you with gamma rays and if you've travelled all that way just to be rude, it would serve you right.

On we go, and each time we have to go further to reach our next planet. This time it's at least 600 million km before we reach the most stunning object in the sky...

SATURN

```
PLANET CHECK LIST:
1. PLANET SURFACE   SIMILAR TO JUPITER.
2. GRAVITY STRENGTH SLIGHTLY MORE
                    THAN EARTH.
3. ATMOSPHERE       MAINLY HYDROGEN
                    WITH SOME HELIUM.
4. PRESSURE         MUCH LESS THAN
                    JUPITER BUT STILL
                    PRETTY GRIM.
5. TEMPERATURE      MINUS 176°.
6. RADIATION        NOT WORTH RISKING.
7. WIND             LETHAL! OVER 1500
                    KM/H IN PLACES - EVEN
                    WORSE THAN JUPITER.
```

Saturn is a bit like Jupiter's baby sister, but nearly twice as far away from the Sun. Trying to land here is certainly not to be recommended, but alternative accommodation is available locally as you will find out.

Saturn is 95 times heavier than Earth and the

surface is yellowish with some darker and lighter coloured belts going round it. It doesn't have the strong features that Jupiter has but Saturn HAS got:

The rings!

If you are looking around the sky with a reasonable telescope, most stars and planets look rather similar. Some are slightly bluer, some are redder, but generally they all appear as little dots of light. Saturn is the one which is different because of its amazing ring system. Other planets have rings but none of them show up like Saturn's.

There are several main rings listed by letters in the order that they were discovered. (A and B are much the brightest so they were spotted first.) The main rings are made up of lots of very thin rings of which there are about 100,000 in total. Each ring is a very long line of rock and ice fragments varying in size from boulders to dust.

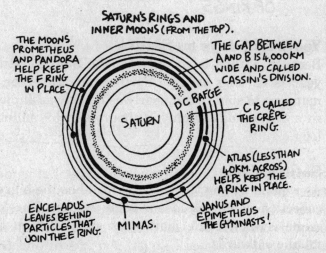

SATURN'S RINGS AND INNER MOONS (FROM THE TOP).

THE MOONS PROMETHEUS AND PANDORA HELP KEEP THE F RING IN PLACE.

THE GAP BETWEEN A AND B IS 4,000 KM WIDE AND CALLED CASSINI'S DIVISION.

C IS CALLED THE CRÊPE RING.

ATLAS (LESS THAN 40 KM. ACROSS) HELPS KEEP THE A RING IN PLACE.

ENCELADUS LEAVES BEHIND PARTICLES THAT JOIN THE E RING.

MIMAS.

JANUS AND EPIMETHEUS THE GYMNASTS!

SATURN

D C B A F G E

- Even though the rings are up to 272,000 km across, in some places they are only a few metres thick! If you could shrink the rings to the size of a football pitch, they would be no thicker than a piece of paper.
- Some of Saturn's moons fly round with the rings and help keep them in position. Moons that do this are called "shepherds".
- About every 15 years the rings disappear! This is because as our view of Saturn moves around the sky, the rings get turned sideways on to us, and they are too thin to see from Earth.

USUAL VIEW OF RINGS

WHEN RINGS ARE SIDEWAYS

Years and days on Saturn

Because Saturn is so far from the Sun, a Saturn year is as long as $29^{1}/_{2}$ Earth years. However, it manages to spin round nearly as quickly as Jupiter, so a Saturn day is only 10 hours and 39 minutes long.

Saturn's sats

As well as having the rings, Saturn has the biggest collection of moons in our solar system. Here's a name check for the main ones starting from the middle outwards:

Atlas · Prometheus · Pandora · Epimetheus
Janus · Mimas · Enceladus · Tethys
Telesto · Calypso · Dione · Helene
Rhea · Titan · Hyperion · Iapetus
Phoebe

Size guide

utterly feeble · a bit weedy · that's more like it

serious contender · titanic

SOME MOON FEATURES:

- Mimas has a crater so big that it looks like an apple with a bite taken out of it.
- Janus and Epimetheus do a bit of cosmic gymnastics. Their orbits are so close to each other that every four years one catches the other up and then they do a funny little twirl and swap positions!
- Tethys, Telesto and Calypso follow each other round in exactly the same path, always staying the same distance apart. Helene and Dione also act as a pair that chase each other.
- Iapetus is white on one side and black on the other.

- Phoebe goes round backwards compared to all the others. It probably used to be an asteroid that got caught by Saturn's gravity.

However, by far the biggest and most interesting moon is...

Titan

Titan is larger than the planet Mercury and is second only to Jupiter's Ganymede in the "Biggest Moon in the Solar System" competition. Best of all there is an extra feature which for years has had scientists jumping up and down in trouser-tiddling excitement ... Titan has an atmosphere! We couldn't breathe it because it is nitrogen and methane, but there's enough of it to give a pressure about 1½ times Earth, which makes us start to seriously wonder – could there be some sort of life?

Titan looks solid enough, so let's land and have a look round.

To start with the sky is obliterated by orange clouds, so sadly we won't be able to see Saturn or the rings. Furthermore, if it rains DO NOT DRINK IT! This is because the rain will not be water but liquid methane. On Earth we use methane gas burners for cooking, but as Titan turns out to be a few degrees colder even than Saturn, methane can be liquid or even in solid lumps.

As for finding life ... well you can have a look but sadly it is just too cold for any life-form that we would recognize or understand. Still, we don't care, we're going to invent our own Titanian anyway.

The Saturnian and Titanian

Saturn is a gas planet like Jupiter, so the Saturnian will also need to be permanently airborne. As the winds storms are so violent the Saturnian will need powerful wings to escape trouble, and several different sets so that they can take turns to rest. Saturn does not have enough radiation to feed on, so the creature will need some way of breathing the hydrogen atmosphere. As hydrogen is pretty useless to live on, it will need to breathe a lot of it, so there will be a massive nose with lots of nostrils. Even though it is flapping away furiously all the time, the temperature is so cold that it will need a fur coat to keep warm, too.

Because of Titan's vast amount of ice and shatteringly low temperatures, the Titanian will need to be some sort of giant cosmic penguin in

order to stay warm enough. The trouble is that even Earth penguins tend to be a bit touchy so a very chilly Titanic penguin is likely to have an extreme attitude problem. If you meet one SERIOUS RESPECT IS DUE.

Since we started out on Mercury we've travelled nearly 1,500 million km to get to Saturn (and remember we've been incredibly lucky that the planets were all in a straight line!) If you were hoping the next journey would be just a quick hop, forget it because we'll have to go another 1,500 million km before we reach the seventh planet from the sun, and the third of the giants...

URANUS

PLANET CHECKLIST:
1. PLANET SURFACE ICE, THICK GAS, LIQUID METHANE. A REAL MESS.

2 GRAVITY STRENGTH	SLIGHTLY MORE THAN EARTH.
3. ATMOSPHERE	HYDROGEN AND HELIUM.
4. PRESSURE	PROBABLY HIGH.
5. TEMPERATURE	WARNING! –216.°
6. RADIATION	NOT A BIG PROBLEM.
7. WIND	MAYBE.

We are now really starting to step into the UNKNOWN. All the planets we've visited so far have been known about for thousands of years; indeed if you go to Italy you can see where the ancient Romans built temples to most of them. Uranus was not discovered until 1781, and so is still a bit of a novelty.

As we approach Uranus you will see that it is a rather fetching bluey-green colour, but don't think about landing. The one thing we do know about this bit of the unknown is that the spaceship will probably just freeze up into a giant methane iceball.

Don't get lost!
Uranus does have a magnetic field but it is not nearly as strong as Earth's. Watch out though because there are three problems about trying to find your way by using a compass.

1 The North Pole and South Pole are not quite on opposite sides of the planet from each other.

2 Your compass will tell you that the North Pole is near the Equator.

3 Scientists think the poles are slowly swapping places with each other!

Weird years and days on Uranus

Uranus takes 84 Earth years to travel right round the sun once and it spins round in 17 hours and 14 minutes. This means that there are over 42,000 Uranian "days" in each year!

Things here are weird because ... Uranus spins on its side!

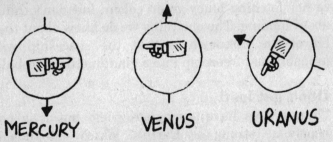

Remember how we found that Venus was spinning backwards? Well Uranus spins sideways. If you had a model of Uranus, instead of spinning from left to right it would spin from top to bottom!

Suppose you lived a few thousand miles from the North Pole of Uranus, and you could see through the thick clouds...

- In summer the Sun would stay in the sky going round and round in circles for nearly 21 Earth years.
- In autumn the Sun would come up and go down once every 17 hours and 14 minutes.
- In winter it would be dark for nearly 21 Earth years.
- In spring the Sun would come up and go down once every 17 hours and 14 minutes ... but it would move in the opposite direction to autumn!

Mind you, the Sun would only look very tiny indeed. Far bigger and much more interesting would be:

The moons of Uranus

For a long time people only knew about the five biggest moons, but in 1986 the spacecraft Voyager 2 found 10 more nearer in to the planet. They all have particularly nice names which come from characters in Shakespeare plays, and so here they are starting with the closest to the planet (this list might come in handy if your cat has kittens and you can't think what to call them): Cordelia, Ophelia, Bianca, Cressida, Desdemona, Juliet, Portia, Rosalind, Belinda, Puck; and the five biggest: Miranda, Ariel, Umbriel, Titania, Oberon. (If you like funny names, then you'll be interested to know that Puck has three big craters called Bogle, Lob and Butz!)

The five big moons are different from each other, and in particular the baby of the bunch, Miranda, has

117

craters, ice cliffs, valleys, plains and everything else to make scientists go all soppy when they look at it.

YOU'RE SO BEAUTIFUL, PLEASE LET'S GET MARRIED. I'M SURE WE'll WORK SOMETHING OUT.

Uranian rings

Yes, there are some thin spooky black rings but after Saturn they aren't really worth a look. The lowest moons, Cordelia and Ophelia, keep them in place, which is just as well because nobody else would want them.

The Uranian creature

If you can't find Uranians at first, look in the rivers of methane. To conserve even the tiniest amount of body heat, the Uranian will have to be MASSIVE like a giant whale, and will need to live in the sea to stop itself falling apart. It will come up to breathe hydrogen through its blow-hole. Even the Titanic Penguin would be spooked out by the Uranian.

We have already travelled at least 2,800 million km since our first stop on Mercury so we are getting the hang of long distances. That's just as well because we have to go another 1,600 million km before we reach...

NEPTUNE

Neptune has a particularly good sign, don't you think?

PLANET CHECK LIST:
1. PLANET SURFACE   STU.
2. GRAVITY STRENGTH   STU.
3. ATMOSPHERE   STU.
4. PRESSURE   STU.
5. TEMPERATURE   STU.
6. RADIATION   MORE THAN U.
7. WIND   WARNING! UP TO
                         1000 KM/H IN PLACES.

"Gosh! What's this?" you eagerly ask. "What does STU mean?"

STU is a secret code that describes nearly everything on Neptune, in fact you've just travelled another billion and a half kilometres to discover a place that is almost completely STU ... Similar To Uranus. There are only a few differences:

● Neptune looks bluer in colour than Uranus.

● Neptune has a large dark spot (a bit like Jupiter's

119

red spot) which is about the size of Earth. It also has a smaller dark spot called The Scooter because it moves round the planet rather quickly!

- Neptune has some nuclear reactions going on in the centre of the planet, which is why the temperature is STU even though the Sun is much further away.
- Neptune has some wicked winds blowing!

Otherwise nearly everything on Neptune is STU including:

- Neptune's magnetic field is nearly as wonky as the one on Uranus.
- Neptune has weedy black rings.
- Neptune has moons.
- Neptune would be very dodgy to land on.

A bad place for birthdays

Neptune takes nearly 165 Earth years to travel right round the sun once, which means Neptune is a rotten place to be born on because you'll never live long enough to have a birthday. It takes about 16 hours to spin round, which means that even Neptune days are STU.

Neptune's moons

Everybody used to think Neptune only had two moons, Triton and Nereid, until Voyager 2 went past and found six more floating lumps big enough to qualify.

At that time scientists had run out of decent names for moons, so starting with the nearest to the planet, here's what they are called:

N6, N5, N4, N3, N2, N1, Triton and Nereid.

Pathetic, wasn't it? It was particularly unfair on N1 because it is a lot bigger than Nereid. (The reason Nereid was originally spotted from Earth and N1 wasn't is that Nereid is about 5 million km away from Neptune, and N1 is only 120,000 km away. Being so far out from Neptune made Nereid easy to detect.)

Photo opportunities

Neptune is extremely pretty and you'll want to get a few snaps of it. The stunning blue planet shines in the sunlight, and the weird dark spots are nicely offset by some white wispy clouds. You might even manage to get the rings in the background – BUT don't use all your film up before you've seen...

Triton

Triton is nearly as big as our own moon and it is by far the largest moon of Neptune. (If Triton was as big as a football, then Neptune's other moons would only be grapes.) It has been described as the most mysterious place in the solar system, and in every way it's the coolest.

- From a distance it looks gorgeous – a fetching blue colour with pinkish ice caps.
- It has an atmosphere! It's only very thin but that's still pretty exclusive for a moon. (Saturn's Titan is the only other moon to have one.)
- The temperature is an extremely cool minus 236° – probably the coldest place in the solar system.

Here are two more especially cool features:

THE ICE VOLCANOES
Triton has active volcanoes, which is also pretty exclusive. (Apart from Earth there are only two other places that have active volcanoes. Can you remember where they were?) With Triton being so cold, you might think volcanoes are good news because you can go and warm your hands on a nice stream of molten lava. DON'T – these volcanoes shoot out liquid nitrogen which smashes itself together into giant lumps of freezing gas! They must look completely awesome.

THE BACKWARD MOON
Triton has what is called a "retrograde orbit". This means it goes round Neptune the wrong way, and for a big moon that's really unusual.

The Neptunian and the Tritonite

Forget bones, skin, blood, eyeballs, fur and so on. At these temperatures any alien would have to be made up purely from electromagnetic energy. So the Neptunian would be just a series of bleeps, maybe with a few gamma rays and a handful of photons thrown in.

The Tritonite must be the same as the Neptunian apart from one thing ... as Triton is 20° colder, the bleeps will be wearing thick anoraks.

Because Neptune and Triton are so stunning, they are bound to be selling postcards and film for your camera.

...AND NEPTUNIAN ACTION FIGURES! (BATTERIES NOT INCLUDED)

Our next journey is a bit of a mystery because we don't know how far we are going. It will probably be about another 1,500 million km, but it could be anything between just a few million and 10,000 million. Let's just hope for the best as we set off for...

PLUTO

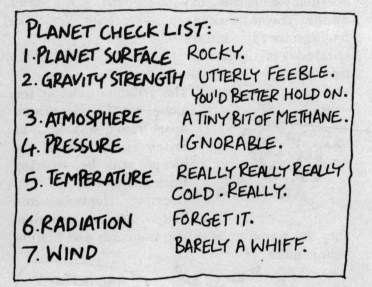

PLANET CHECK LIST:
1. PLANET SURFACE   ROCKY.
2. GRAVITY STRENGTH   UTTERLY FEEBLE.
                     YOU'D BETTER HOLD ON.
3. ATMOSPHERE   A TINY BIT OF METHANE.
4. PRESSURE   IGNORABLE.
5. TEMPERATURE   REALLY REALLY REALLY COLD. REALLY.
6. RADIATION   FORGET IT.
7. WIND   BARELY A WHIFF.

You've come a long way for this, but it has to be said, Pluto is not Disneyland. It is smaller than our moon and a dull yellow colour. As you land, there is a strange splattery squelching sound.

URGH! WHAT IS IT?!

Don't panic, it's just the Pluto creature hurrying up to see you.

Because Pluto's gravity is so weak, the Pluton has to cling to the ground all the time. It looks like a slug which leaves a gooey trail to stick itself down, and it is covered in suckers for extra grip. The lack of pressure means its body billows about like a half inflated plastic sack, but the main thing you notice is that the tears in its phenomenally large eyes indicate that it is pitifully pleased to see you.

"Please stay," snuffles the creature, which has a giant nose to make the most of the almost non-existent atmosphere. You can't help shuddering because the nose is permanently running due to the cold.

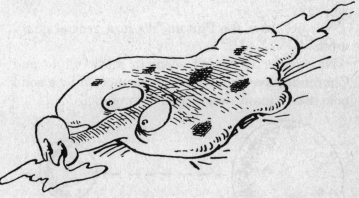

"All right," you say. "What is there to do here?"

"Look at that big star," says the Pluton.

You see that one yellowish star in the sky does seem to be brighter than the others, and suddenly you realize that it is the Sun. You do a fantastically quick mental calculation and work out that Pluto takes 247 Earth years to make just one journey right round it.

"We've got a moon too," says the Pluton.

"That must be more interesting," you say to be polite.

"Let's watch it," says the Pluton. "It's called Charon."

You look up, and for a moment you are impressed. Charon isn't much smaller than Pluto itself – in fact if it was a moon of Saturn it would qualify for a "serious contender" rating as it is 1,200 km across. Unfortunately, after a whole Pluto day (which is nearly as long as an Earth week) you find you are really bored.

"Doesn't your moon move round the sky at all?" you say.

"Oh no," says the Pluton, "it's in a geostationary orbit."

No wonder it doesn't seem to move. Pluto and Charon behave as if they were connected by a solid pole (like a giant weightlifter's dumb-bell).

CHARON

PLUTO

While you are wondering where the Pluton came across a word like "geostationary", the creature makes a suggestion:

126

"If you like we can go round to the other side of the planet and we won't see Charon at all."

"That sounds like too much excitement for me," you say. "But tell me, how come the last four planets I've been to are gassy giants, and this is just a little rock?"

"We weren't always part of the solar system," explains the Pluton. "We were just flying through space and got caught up by the yellow star's gravity and here we still are."

"A-ha!" you say cleverly. You have just realized why you didn't know how far you were going to have to travel to get from Neptune to Pluto.

When Pluto latched onto the solar system, it came in at a funny angle and ended up going round the sun in an ellipse shape. This means Pluto very gradually moves in and out from the sun, and between the years 1979 and 1999 Pluto has actually been closer to the sun than Neptune.

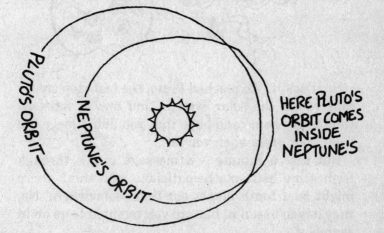

PLUTO'S ORBIT

NEPTUNE'S ORBIT

HERE PLUTO'S ORBIT COMES INSIDE NEPTUNE'S

"What else is there to see?" you ask.

"Oh! Er, lots and lots..." says the Pluton desperately.

"Oh dear," you sigh as you realize that you have already exhausted all the thrills that Pluto has to offer. Here comes the most difficult part of the trip so far – you have to somehow make an excuse for leaving the sad little Pluton that never gets any visitors. You brace yourself for what is bound to be a tearful scene, but then...

"Ah-ah-AH-TISHOOOOO...!"

You look on in amazement as the Pluton helplessly blasts off into space. The crippling temperature and feeble gravity have finally taken their toll and the creature has sneezed itself right off the planet.

So that's it. We reached Pluto, the last stop on our tour round the solar system, and now it must be time to get home and hope that you didn't leave the front door open when you left.

But just a minute – a message comes through from some astro-mathematicians who think there might be a tenth planet out there somewhere! No, they haven't seen it, but are you tempted to go on in search of...

PLANET X

PLANET CHECK LIST:
PLEASE FILL THIS IN WHEN YOU GET THERE!
1. PLANET SURFACE —
2. GRAVITY STRENGTH —
3. ATMOSPHERE —
4. PRESSURE —
5. TEMPERATURE —
6. RADIATION —
7. WIND —

Why do they think there might be a Planet X?

ALL THE PLANETS OUT TO SATURN HAD BEEN KNOWN ABOUT FOR THOUSANDS OF YEARS. THEN SUDDENLY IN 1781 . . . . .

HEY! I'VE FOUND ANOTHER PLANET!

Good luck, then!

WELCOME TO DEEP SPACE!

So far everything in this book has been nice and normal. We've looked up at the sky, we've flown about a bit and seen a few planets, we've visited hot places, cold places and extremely freezing places, but generally nothing too weird has happened.

The hard thing to understand is that even though we covered at least 6,000 million km getting to Pluto, in terms of space we are still in our own backyard.

The nearest star to our sun (which is called Proxima Centauri) is 40 million million km away which is more than 6,500 times further away than Pluto! Of course writing out numbers such as 40,000,000,000,000 gets very irritating after a while, so astronomers have a neater way of describing massive distances.

Light years

Did you know that light travels at 300,000 km per second?

When you turn a light on, you might think that you see it immediately but you would be wrong. The light has to travel from the bulb to your eye, but because it travels so fast it seems to be immediate.

You don't realize light has to travel when you are dealing with short distances but for long distances it starts to make a difference. Here's how long it takes light to reach us from different places:

The Moon	$1\frac{1}{4}$ seconds
The Sun	8 minutes 20 seconds
Neptune	over 4 hours
The nearest star	4.3 YEARS!

● This means that if the sun suddenly exploded, we wouldn't see it for 8 minutes and 20 seconds – plenty of time to find some very dark glasses.

Astronomers use light years to describe how far away stars are. If the light from a star takes 10 years to reach us they say it is 10 light years away.
● One light year is 9,500,000 million km (or 5,900,000 million miles).

Because stars are so far away, it makes travel to them seem impossible. Remember the space probe Voyager 2 took twelve years to reach Neptune? If it could keep going at the same speed, to reach the nearest star would take over 90,000 years.

However, due to some very peculiar laws of physics it might just be possible to visit other stars, but before we do let's find out more about them.

The life of a star, or Dwarves and giants

It all starts with the very simplest thing in the universe: hydrogen gas. Massive clouds of hydrogen gather, together with space dust which has come from old stars that have been and gone. (These clouds are billions of kilometres across.) A cloud like this is called a NEBULA and it acts as a nursery for raising baby stars.

To begin with all stars form the same way. The effect of gravity gradually causes the particles in the nebula to move in closer to each other. As they do so, a lump forms which keeps getting bigger and thicker and the lump's gravity gets stronger and stronger. As the particles in the middle start to get squashed, the lump gets hotter and hotter and gradually it turns into a baby star. What happens next depends on how big the baby is.

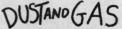

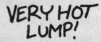

If the baby star isn't big enough ... nothing happens and gradually it all cools off and gives up. This is called a BROWN DWARF.

If there is enough gas involved, the temperature in the middle will top 10,000,000°C and this triggers a nuclear reaction. Hydrogen starts getting turned into helium in a process which gives off masses of heat and light. A star is born!

There are a few ways a star might spend its life, and again this depends on how big it is to start with.

Small stars

This is the life story of all stars smaller than our sun, and those that are slightly bigger.

1 The star will have enough hydrogen to burn for up to about 10 billion years.
  ● Our sun is about halfway through its fuel supply.
  ● The amount of heat and light that comes from a star depends on how much weight it loses in converting the hydrogen to helium. Our sun loses 4,000,000 tonnes every second!

2 Towards the end of this time the hydrogen starts running out and different things happen. The very centre of the star will shrink and get hotter while the outside expands and cools off. From far away the star will look very big and red, and it gets called a RED GIANT. When our own sun finally swells up like this, Earth and everything on it will be zapped to bits.

3 A red giant does not last long. It might explode in which case it is called a NOVA. Otherwise it might gradually fade back to a hot centre surrounded by gas and this is a PLANETARY NEBULA. (Planetary nebula is a confusing name because it has nothing to do with planets!)

4 Soon the centre core is left on its own and this is a WHITE DWARF. White dwarfs are very small but very heavy – a mug full of white dwarf material would weigh 10 tonnes! They are like people who spend too long sunbathing – extremely hot but not very bright.

5 Eventually a white dwarf will cool down to become a BLACK DWARF, but we don't know if the universe is old enough for any black dwarves to have appeared yet. They are certainly too small, dark, far away and generally too feeble for us to see.

Big stars

Stars bigger than 1.4 times the size of our sun have a different life.

1 The star burns up its hydrogen faster. Really big stars might do this in a few million years. Towards the end it becomes a RED SUPERGIANT.

2 When the fuel burns out everything suddenly stops and the star collapses until a mugful of this stuff would weigh at least ten thousand million tonnes! The temperature shoots up to a hundred thousand *million*°C and then, not surprisingly, it blows itself to bits. This outburst is called a SUPERNOVA and it can release more energy in a few seconds than our sun does in millions of years. Supernova outbursts can look amazing from Earth, but sadly they only happen a few times every century.

3 After the supernova has died away, what is left is called a NEUTRON STAR which is only about 20 km across.

● A neutron star is a really depressing place to visit if you are on a diet. The gravity is so strong that you would weigh about five million million kg.

4 The neutron star spins round and sends out pulses of radio waves, which is why neutron stars are sometimes called PULSARS.

5 Eventually the pulsar slows down, stops and gives up.

Really big stars

If a star is more than three times bigger than the sun (and some of them are hundreds of times bigger) then the ending is even more bizarre.

1 The star burns up all its fuel and has a SUPER-NOVA outburst.

2 The star collapses and keeps collapsing and keeps collapsing...

3 ... the star squashes into itself so much that the fabric of the atoms breaks apart, time stops, and the most peculiar object in the universe is created. Although it might be just a few kilometres across it is heavier than a neutron star, it is... A BLACK HOLE!

Colours of stars: Although most stars look white, they can range from steely blue to deep red. The colour mainly depends on how hot they are. We've already seen that the constellation of Orion has both an orange-red star and a blue star. The most feeble stars are tiny little burnt out wrecks called red dwarves.

What is a black hole?

Yes indeed, you've heard stories, you've heard rumours, people have guessed, people have pondered BUT nobody has ever seen one!

The easiest way to imagine a black hole is to think of the greediest bloke in the world. He is so hungry he eats everything that comes near him ... and even eats himself until he disappears! A black hole is doing the same sort of thing, it has such a strong gravity that it sucks everything that comes too near into itself ... even including light. Because it sucks light in, that means you can't see it.

How do we know they are there?

When really clever scientists like Albert Einstein and Stephen Hawking worked out how the universe was put together, there were a few details that needed to be sorted out. They realized that BLACK HOLES had to exist to complete their theories. Although nobody can see black holes, their gravity is so strong that they affect stars and other objects around them. When distant stars seem to move in strange ways, it can often be explained by a nearby black hole pulling them about.

How to have fun with a black hole

If ever you come across a black hole, there is a good experiment you can play. You need:
- A big clock that you can see a long way away.
- Somebody called Sid who won't mind falling into a parallel universe.

Make sure you are standing WELL BACK from the black hole yourself, a few billion billion kilometres should be enough.

1 Give Sid a big clock to hold.

TICK
TICK
TICK

2 Make him walk towards the EVENT HORIZON of

the black hole. (Event horizon is what the edge is called.)

3 Watch the clock. As Sid gets closer, you will see the clock go slower and slower, and as Sid reaches the horizon it will stop. This is because for an observer (i.e. you) the black hole slows time down. The really odd thing is that Sid will think the clock is still working perfectly!

4 Say goodbye for ever to Sid.

By now Sid will have been sucked into the centre. Each atom in his body will be pulled to an infinite length and will be infinitesimally thin as he passes through a space singularity. What happens after that is anybody's guess, but some people think that he might emerge in another universe. Mind you, he probably wouldn't look too well.

You probably want to know what a singularity is, don't you? Oh dear. It takes a bit of imagining, but it's a tiny point where everything comes together, and to fit it all into this tiny point everything has to be squashed down to an infinitesimally small size. Think about trying to squash an elephant into a matchbox and that will give you a rough idea for starters.

One way of understanding a singularity is to make one using sums. Pick your favourite number, then divide it by zero. What do you get? (The answer is that you'll probably get a headache.)

Size comparisons

Here are some examples of the diameters of dwarves and giants. ("Diameter" means how far it is across.)

Our sun	1,400,000 km
Red giant	300,000,000 km
Red supergiant	500,000,000 km
White dwarf	3,000 km
Pulsar	20 km
Black hole:	
Event horizon	10km
Centre	less than a pin point.

● Remember ... despite their smaller sizes, a pulsar is heavier than a white dwarf and a black hole is the heaviest of all.

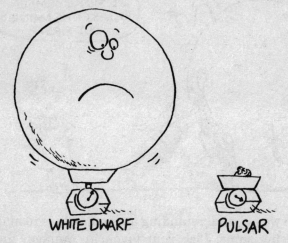

WHITE DWARF   PULSAR

So how does a black hole stop time and bend light? The answer is thanks to the laws of...

Relativity

In the late 1600s a brilliant mathematician called
Isaac Newton answered lots of questions about how
planets and stars move with his theories of how
gravity works. His ideas were so good that
absolutely everything fitted in with them ... except
there was a tiny discrepancy in the orbit of Mercury.
Nobody could explain this until about 1900 when an
office clerk in Germany started thinking about it.
This office clerk turned out to be the mentally
mighty Albert Einstein.

Albert chopped up, sorted out, repainted, plugged
in and switched on Isaac's ideas and came up with
his GENERAL THEORY OF RELATIVITY. There
are only about twenty or thirty people in the whole
world who can understand how he worked it all out,
but luckily for us we can just look at the results.

These include some real mind bending gems such as:
- Curved space.
- Time warping.
- $E = mc^2$. This is the equation that says how much energy you get if something disappears, which is what happens in nuclear reactions like the sun burning up. E is the energy, m is the amount of stuff you lose and c is the speed of light. Easy!
- The weight of light. Yes! Light does weigh a tiny amount. The weight of light hitting the Earth in one second is about 3kg. If distant star light comes past something with a lot of gravity like a black hole, the light can be bent!

One of the main things about relativity is that NOTHING CAN GO FASTER THAN THE SPEED OF LIGHT – which is 300,000 km per second.

Albert Einstein worked out that all sorts of odd things start happening when you start travelling closer and closer to the speed of light.
- Time for you would slow down.
- You would get heavier.
- Anybody watching you would think you had got thinner.
- Your hat would blow off.

The oddest effect is the slowing down of time, but this has actually been measured. When the first astronauts went to the Moon, there was a very accurate clock on their rocket and another one back on Earth. Because the rocket had been moving at several thousand kilometres per hour, by the time it got back they found that the rocket clock was a few seconds behind the clock on Earth.

- While the rocket had been moving, time in the rocket had slowed down.
- This means that the astronauts were a few seconds younger than if they had stayed on Earth.
- Time can also be slowed down by strong gravity. The Sun is much bigger than the Earth, and so has much stronger gravity. If you have two absolutely accurate clocks, one on the Sun and one on Earth, the Sun clock would run slower – it would lose about 1 second every six days.

The faster you go, the more time slows down for you, and if you travel at the speed of light time will stop completely.

- There is one very good proof that it is impossible to travel backwards in time – nobody from the future has been to visit us!

Hey! Wait a minute ...

if time can be slowed down by travelling VERY FAST INDEED

...maybe we could visit other stars billions of kilometres away without getting too old on the journey!

All we have to do is make sure our rocket is moving fast enough, so as you were promised at the start of this book, let's go...

ACROSS THE HORIZON OF TIME

The main thing we will need is a rocket that can travel for ages at almost the speed of light. Is it possible? Maybe it is with...

The anti-matter drive

At the moment rockets are propelled by the effect of fuel burning and shooting out of the back, but just recently scientists have developed a few atoms of "anti-matter".

Anti-stuff is the opposite of the normal stuff out of which everything is made. If you mix anti-stuff with normal stuff they cancel each other out and disappear! However, when they disappear they release a MEGA amount of energy. (So if you stand too close, you'll be stuffed.) This means that a tiny bit of anti-stuff (or anti-matter for that matter) would keep a rocket powered up for thousands of years. So why haven't we done it already?

● Anti-matter is extremely difficult to make.
● What do you keep it in?

Have faith. Scientists love solving problems like this, so maybe we'll get our super rocket after all.

Our first journey at almost the speed of light

Let's go and visit SIRIUS, the dog star, which is the brightest star in our sky and is about 8½ light years away. Pack up some sandwiches then hop into the rocket, wave goodbye to everybody and BLAST OFF. Thanks to the anti-matter drive we are soon travelling very close to the speed of light, so it takes us 8½ years to get there.

● When we reach Sirius we see a little white dwarf star that spins around with it. This little star is rather cutely called the PUP, and when we get back we'll read the next few pages of this book to find out what these two are up to.

Take a few snaps for the album, turn round and 8½ years later we get home again. The journey has taken us 17 years ... OR HAS IT?

● Because we were moving at almost the speed of light, time for us on the rocket had slowed right down! Apart from when we lost speed by taking off and landing, on board the rocket we might have only noticed a few minutes pass. During the total journey of 161,000,000,000,000 km we might not even have had time to eat our sandwiches!

● Time on Earth did not slow down, so your friends all think you have been away for 17 years. If you do have some sandwiches left over, they will be amazed that they have not gone mouldy.

● If you had a twin sister when you set off, she would be 17 years older than you when you got back.

● If you were 16 when you set off, and had just had a baby boy, by the time you got back, your son would be older than you!

147

Right then, now you've got the hang of light speed travel, let's really see some space!

- Before you set off, clear any cheese or milk out of your fridge. Even if the trip only seems like a few hours to you, thousands of Earth years will pass before you get back again. Imagine what the inside of the fridge would look like then. Ugh.

The last big trip: What will we find?

As we go through deep space, we are going to get a close up view of some wonderful things.

Double stars

SIRIUS with its companion dwarf star, the PUP, is called a double star. The Pup is far fainter, but like all white dwarves it's very heavy. The two stars are held in orbit round each other by their gravities and spin round once every 50 years.

Pairs of stars like this are extremely common, and lead to even more complicated arrangements. The constellation of Gemini features two main stars, CASTOR and POLLUX and from Earth you can see that Pollux is orange and Castor is white. However, Castor isn't quite what it seems.

Castor is actually made up of six stars all close together. They spin round as two normal double stars and one pair of faint dwarf stars.

The Demon Star!

The constellation of Perseus features an amazing star ALGOL, or "The Demon Star". Algol burns quite brightly for 59 hours, but then fades down for 5 hours until it is about ¼ of its usual strength. It then takes 5 hours to fade back up again.

Algol is actually a double star, each of which is about 2½ million km across, and they are 10 million km apart. As they spin round they keep blocking each other's light from the Earth, and so the double system appears dimmer.

The disappearing constellations

The constellations were made up by grouping together bunches of stars which look close together in the sky. This is a bit misleading though, because some of the stars in a constellation might be much further away from us than others.

Have a look at Ursa Major:

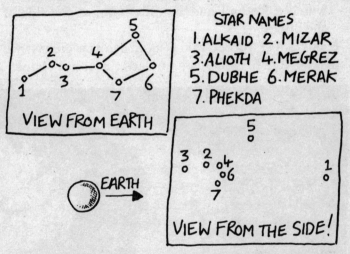

STAR NAMES
1. ALKAID 2. MIZAR
3. ALIOTH 4. MEGREZ
5. DUBHE 6. MERAK
7. PHEKDA

VIEW FROM EARTH

EARTH

VIEW FROM THE SIDE!

When you go to fly among the stars in a constellation, the pattern will disappear! Although Alkaid and Mizar look close together in the sky, Alkaid is 210 light years away from Earth, but Mizar is only 88 light years away.

The rest of our galaxy

- Our galaxy is about 100,000 light years across and contains about a million million stars, one of which is our Sun.
- Our galaxy is in the shape of a flat spiral which is spinning round.
- Our Sun is about 30,000 light years from the centre of the galaxy and it takes about 225 million years to spin right round it once.
- All the stars you can see from Earth are the very nearest neighbours to us in our own galaxy.
- From Earth the only way to see the rest of our galaxy is to look up at the Milky Way, but we only get a sideways on view. It's a bit like trying to watch a football match while lying at the side of the pitch.

If our super rocket takes us above the galaxy, we will be able to look down and see the spiral shape.

In the middle are a mass of old red giants, and out along the two arms are a mixture of old and new stars. We (on Earth) are about halfway along one of the arms.

Our galaxy is one of a small local group which contains about 20–30 galaxies all within a few million light years of each other. Our galaxy and the Andromeda galaxy are the two biggest.

- Andromeda is also a spiral galaxy, but there are other types, such as elliptical and irregular. (Mind you, spiral galaxies are definitely the coolest looking galaxies to be living in.)

Clusters and super clusters

Groups of galaxies bunch together to form "clusters" which can contain thousands of galaxies. Our local group is on the outskirts of the Virgo cluster, the middle of which is about 60 million light years away.

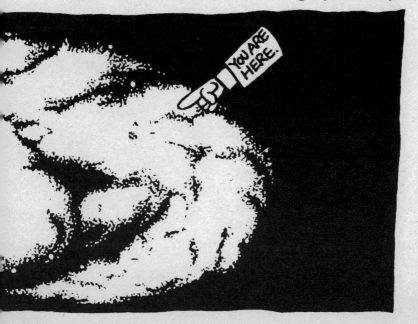

(It's called the Virgo cluster because the main body of it can be detected in the direction of the constellation of Virgo.)

● If an alien with a VERY powerful telescope looked at Earth today from the other side of the Virgo cluster, he would see the dinosaurs! The light from Earth would have taken over 65 million years to reach him, so he would see what was happening here over 65 million years ago.

Clusters string themselves into long ribbons called superclusters, and superclusters arrange themselves a bit like the strands of an old cobweb leaving massive empty spaces in the middle. One of these arrangements of superclusters has been called "The Great Wall" and it stretches over half a billion light years across space.

● By now you will be getting a bit numbed by all these big numbers of light years, so let's remind ourselves exactly how long this Great Wall is: 5,000,000,000,000,000,000,000,000 km.

So what have we learnt from this? The main thing is that if we get lost in space, we ought to know our home address.

The Natives,
Earth,
The Solar System,
The Milky Way Galaxy,
The Local Group,
Near the Virgo Cluster,
Just off The Great Wall,
The Universe.

Getting near the edge...

Still travelling near light speed, we are now 1½ billion light years away from Earth and we are meeting some completely new objects:

Quasars

Quasars are very bright and are blasting out radio waves so strongly that they can be detected from Earth. Why do you think they are so powerful? Is it because...

1 They are new galaxies exploding into existence.

2 They are lots of black holes discharging their energy.

3 A whole pile of matter has met up with some anti-matter.

The answer is probably number 1 but at the moment nobody knows, so you can make up your own idea.

● Remember Sid who stepped into the black hole for us? Maybe he'll turn up here. What do you think?

There is ONE thing we are fairly sure about quasars, they are all rushing away from us at nearly the speed of light and even in our super rocket we are not going to be able to overtake them.

The most distant quasars we have seen have been over 12 billion light years away and it has been calculated they must be near the edge of the universe. Scientists have also worked out that the universe is about 15 billion years old.

The Big Bang

Scientists are starting to agree that the whole universe began as an extremely tiny little nothing which went BANG...

15 billion years ago	THE BIG BANG
10 billion years ago	Galaxies like the Milky Way were evolved
5 billion years ago	Our solar system got started

...and ever since then the universe has been expanding.

BUT some scientists think that the universe cannot go on getting bigger and bigger for ever. Imagine that every particle in the universe is attached to the middle by a piece of elastic. (This includes our super rocket ... we cannot fly beyond the edge. Sorry about that.) When the elastic is stretched as far as it will go, it will stop stretching and start to pull back. In fact...

in a few billion years	the universe stops expanding
in 10 billion years	the universe starts shrinking
in 15 billion years	the universe collapses
in 20 billion years	THE BIG SPLATT

Yes, in the same way that the biggest stars collapse into the smallest object, the universe is SO MASSIVE that it will disappear into absolutely nothing.

Cheer up ... we don't expect it just yet.

And finally, the big question:

Is there other life out there?

You can't have a book about planets, stars, galaxies, space and everything without wondering about it, so what's the answer?

So far we think there's a chance that some sort of tiny life existed on Mars millions of years ago, but what about now? The universe must have billions and billions of other little planets, so surely Earth cannot be the only one with life on it.

Scientists spend ages doing equations and working out the probabilities of other life, but the answer to the question is far easier than that...

WHY NOT?

155

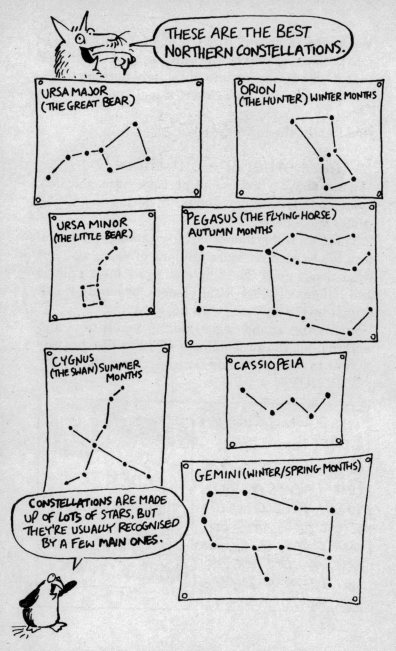

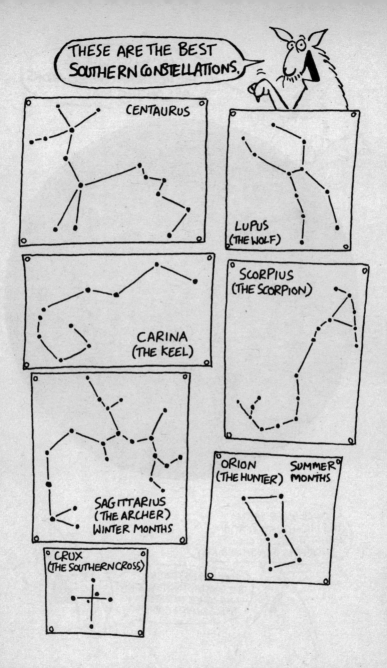